"Wisdom is something we all need. How do we get it? Seek, do, develop, avoid, become. This is so clear and accessible to all. With stirring stories, Raymond Harris models how we can more effectively grow in grace and truth."

—JACK ALEXANDER, CEO, CEO Forum; movie producer

"Raymond Harris has written a deeply thoughtful reflection on the Proverbs that eloquently integrates God's truth with real-life experience in the rough-and-tumble of marketplace realities. As one of America's premier architects, Harris has walked the walk for more than thirty years."

—DR. MAC PIER, president, New York City Leadership Center;
author of *Consequential Leadership*

"There are no theoretical situations in this book. Raymond Harris uses his experiences to show exactly how Solomon's wisdom applies to today's business world. That's why young professionals should read it cover to cover. Give this to every new college graduate who wants to be truly successful."

—DAVE RINER, executive director, Student Mobilization

"Here is a practical book on how to conduct life and business, written by a man who has sought after and lived the book of Proverbs. Profit from its contents and application in your life!"

—BOB DOLL, senior advisor to BlackRock

"Desiring a heart of wisdom, Raymond Harris has lived out Proverbs for years in his life and business. This is not your typical how-to-succeed, self-help book but rather a text springing from intimacy with God and His Word and a heart to obey what God reveals. *The Heart of Business* is both challenging and motivating and will indeed help you succeed in God's economy and kingdom."

—MIKE TRENEER, international president, The Navigators

"*The Heart of Business* is saturated with wise principles. I have gained a more thorough understanding of the book of Proverbs while obtaining wisdom for growth in my own faith and leadership. This is a helpful guide for any leader."

— JENA LEE NARDELLA, founder and president, Blood:Water Mission

"We are defined by the choices we make. Having a tool set to make wise decisions is an absolute must. *The Heart of Business* is just that for me. It's a book that is easy to remember and comprehend and has become a road map for me as I strive to make great decisions in life."

— JON ERWIN, movie writer, producer, director

"Raymond Harris applies the book of Proverbs to real-life business experiences, revealing for us how the Word of God can guide our lives. This is a great book for everyone in the workplace."

— D. G. ELMORE, chairman, Elmore Companies, Inc.;
vice chairman, The Navigators

"How can a young leader keep his or her footing in the world of business? Raymond Harris answers that question. *The Heart of Business* combines godly wisdom from Proverbs with actual scenarios that have been hammered out over four decades of successful business leadership. My son, a recent college graduate, describes Raymond's book as 'solid — just what I need.' I highly recommend it."

— KEN COCHRUM, vice president, student-led and
virtually led movements, Cru

"This book will be especially appealing to international students looking for moral and ethical guidelines in today's global marketplace. You will gain valuable insights into the Proverbs and learn how to be successful while still bringing honor and glory to God."

— DOUG SHAW, president/CEO, International Students, Inc.

THE HEART OF
BUSINESS

SOLOMON'S WISDOM FOR
SUCCESS IN ANY ECONOMY

RAYMOND H. HARRIS

NAVPRESS

Discipleship Inside Out®

NavPress is the publishing ministry of The Navigators, an international Christian organization and leader in personal spiritual development. NavPress is committed to helping people grow spiritually and enjoy lives of meaning and hope through personal and group resources that are biblically rooted, culturally relevant, and highly practical.

For a free catalog go to www.NavPress.com
or call 1.800.366.7788 in the United States or 1.800.839.4769 in Canada.

NavPress titles may be purchased in bulk for ministry, educational, business, fund-raising, or sales promotional use. For information, please call NavPress Special Markets at 1.800.504.2924.

ISBN-13: 978-1-61291-468-8

Cover design by Arvid Wallen

Some of the anecdotal illustrations in this book are true to life and are included with the permission of the persons involved. All other illustrations are composites of real situations, and any resemblance to people living or dead is coincidental.

Unless otherwise identified, all Scripture quotations in this publication are taken from the *Holy Bible, New International Version*® (NIV®). Copyright © 1973, 1978, 1984, 2011 by Biblica, Inc. ®, used by permission of Zondervan. All rights reserved worldwide. The "NIV" and "New International Version" are trademarks registered in the United States Patent and Trademark Office by Biblica, Inc.® Other versions used include: the New American Standard Bible® (NASB), Copyright © 1960, 1962, 1963, 1968, 1971, 1972, 1973, 1975, 1977, 1995 by The Lockman Foundation. Used by permission; the New King James Version (NKJV). Copyright © 1982 by Thomas Nelson, Inc. Used by permission. All rights reserved; and the *Holy Bible*, New Living Translation (NLT), copyright © 1996, 2004, 2007 by Tyndale House Foundation. Used by permission of Tyndale House Publishers, Inc., Carol Stream, Illinois 60188. All rights reserved.

Harris, Raymond H., 1955-
   The heart of business : Solomon's wisdom for success in any economy / Raymond H. Harris.
      pages cm
   ISBN 978-1-61291-468-8
1. Businesspeople--Religious life. 2. Businesspeople--Conduct of life. 3. Business--Religious aspects--Christianity. 4. Business ethics. 5. Bible. Proverbs--Criticism, interpretation, etc. I. Title.
   BV4596.B8H29 2013
   658.4'092--dc23

                                   2013007516

Printed in the United States of America

1 2 3 4 5 6 7 8 / 18 17 16 15 14 13

CONTENTS

ACKNOWLEDGMENTS

This book would not have been possible without my faithful assistant, Lisa Vasquez, and the skillful editing of Steve Gardner and Liz Heaney.

I would like to dedicate this book to my children, Libby Black and Timothy Harris, for whom I have prayed for wisdom since their infancy. I am inadequate without the partnership and faithfulness of my dear wife, Marydel, who sharpens, encourages, and challenges me in my walk with God.

CHAPTER 1

OPERATING A BUSINESS IN GOD'S ECONOMY

My brain told my body to be calm, but it refused to listen. I kept taking deep breaths and forcing myself to at least *look* calm. In twenty-five years of practice I had never been sued. My architectural firm had a spotless record and a well-deserved reputation for excellence. And here I was in the hot seat, trying desperately to keep the firm from collapsing—all because of a collapsed roof that wasn't our fault.

I'll never forget the day the certified letter came. Certified mail has always made me nervous. I suppose it can carry good news as well as bad, but it rarely seems to work that way. Especially when it comes from an attorney I don't recognize. Bad news doesn't get any better with age, and I knew I shouldn't delay opening the letter any longer. Probably a lot of fuss over nothing, anyway.

When I opened the letter, two things struck me immediately. First, the word "DEFENDANT" attached to my name. In neon letters. Second, the word "PLAINTIFF" attached to the name of my major client. This client had accounted for most of my firm's business for over twenty years, and suddenly their insurance subrogation unit was suing me. Not a good sign.

I thought back to a phone call a year earlier. Working on a project in Fairbanks, Alaska, I returned to my hotel one evening to find a red flashing light on the telephone. The desk clerk said, "Yes, Mr. Harris, I have a message for you. Your office called and said you should call right away."

I called immediately, hoping I could still catch someone, but it was too late—three time zones too late. I dialed Ted Schwink at home, and he picked up immediately.

"I hate to tell you this," he said, "but the roof on one of our buildings collapsed in a rainstorm."

I could feel my pulse rising. "Oh, no! Was anyone hurt?"

"I don't know yet. It was pretty bad. The store was completely flooded. Even cars in the parking lot floated away."

"This is a disaster!" I said, as if he didn't already know.

"Yeah," he said. "I've got a flight first thing in the morning so I can see it for myself and figure out what to do next. I still can't believe the roof just collapsed. Even with all that rain. It doesn't make sense."

"No, it doesn't," I said. "Call me as soon as you know something."

Sleep didn't come easily that night. I envisioned a store filled with floating merchandise. How could this have happened?

Our building designs require a significant margin of safety; they should withstand the perfect storm and live to brag about it.

Ted called the next afternoon. "I think we've found the problem. It looks like the water couldn't exit the roof fast enough. It built up like a huge pond on the back loading dock area, and the weight was more than the roof could hold. Thank God no one was hurt. One guy had to jump out of the way to miss the falling debris."

"How did so much water come off the roof at once and wipe out everything below it?"

"No, it didn't collapse like that. Most of the water on the roof didn't actually come inside. In fact, most of the water damage was from the sprinkler system that went off when the roof gave way. But still, all the merchandise was ruined. It's a huge loss."

I was stunned. Millions of dollars in merchandise wasn't the only loss. Lost sales and profits during the time the store would be out of commission, the cost of repairs—large numbers flashed through my mind. Could we be liable? Was our design flawed?

I made an emergency call to an engineer and requested a hydrology study to determine the cause of the collapse. Was the roof drainage system adequate? Did we design large enough scupper holes in the back wall to permit roof water to exit at a fast enough rate?

After a careful study of our drawings, the engineer assured me the design was more than adequate to prevent what happened. His conclusion was that the construction must have deviated from the plans. His confidence gave me a great deal of relief, but I knew it would be an uphill battle to convince our client we were not to blame. The contractor, of course, would do his best to prove that he followed our specifications exactly. The attorneys would "prove" whatever they thought they could get away with. Our major client, the victim, would be protected to some degree by insurance, but the insurer was on the hook for a lot of money—money they would rightly want to recover.

A year later the certified letter showed up, along with a lump in my throat. Six months after the letter, my business partner and I were sitting in a mediation hearing, trying to defend twenty-five years of hard work and countless all-nighters building the firm I started at age twenty-seven. All of it at risk, including the fifty-plus families depending on the firm for their livelihoods.

I felt vulnerable with no script to follow and no idea what the outcome would be. My mind was locked in a spin cycle of two questions: Why am I here? What have I done to deserve this? I kept telling myself I had applied God's principles in building this business. I was confident God had revealed to me those principles, along with many promises, from the pages of Scripture. Had they been enough? These were serious circumstances, and I was definitely not the one in control.

I silently cried out to the Lord for protection many times through the long day of intermittent meetings with numerous attorneys. I had long before given up any hope that the case would be dismissed. The contractor had dug in, and the insurance company needed to find someone at fault—someone with deep enough pockets to pay an award without going bankrupt.

We had designed the store and, of course, the roof as well. Fortunately, no one had been injured, but the thoughts of what *could* have happened were unbearable. Just facing the potential ramifications of what *did* happen made me nauseous.

We had provided professional architectural services for this client for over twenty years. Our diligence and faithfulness should have entered into this case, right? After all, we had produced literally thousands of projects without a single problem; how could this one incident ruin all we had done? Again I cried out to the Lord, asking for his protection.

So why am I telling you this? What do this mediation hearing and lawsuit against our firm have to do with this book? Because it was during those moments of darkness that I truly internalized a huge truth: God *does* protect—regardless of immediate outcomes. God's principles apply to operating a successful business, even in the most dire circumstances.

Is it possible to operate a successful business in accordance with the book of Proverbs? Absolutely! When businessmen and women apply and follow its wisdom, their hearts are transformed to operate their business by the laws of God's economy.

GOD'S ECONOMY VERSUS THE WORLD'S ECONOMY

Two opposing forces compete for our allegiance. Like the epic battle between good and evil or between the eternal and the temporal, these forces battle for our hearts. The Bible says we must choose the master we will serve: either God or money (Matthew 6:24).

Those who settle for money operate according to the world's economy and find themselves enslaved to it. Those who choose God pursue his economy and submit to his ownership, making "sacrifices" that bring freedom and contentment. Their hearts and minds are transformed, shifting away from serving money and possessions toward loving God and seeking true treasures that can never be lost.

In the world's economy people are defined by what they have accomplished. In God's economy, they are defined by who they have become as a result of God's transformation of their hearts. God values what we bring to heaven, not the material wealth and possessions we leave on earth. We certainly cannot take our possessions with us to heaven; however, we can take the great treasures stored inside the heart. These are the things that define us apart from what we have accomplished or accumulated.

God wants us to be fully devoted to his instruction. He wants our hearts, not simply our actions. If we seek to change only our behaviors, we will exhaust ourselves trying to live up to standards we can never achieve. But if we seek him first, we will be transformed, and our actions will follow. The book of Proverbs focuses on instructing the heart. By helping us develop submissive hearts, it points us toward Christ. I have seen its principles and wisdom hold up over time, proving again and again that there is no better business textbook than Proverbs.

THE PREMIER BUSINESS TEXTBOOK

While occasionally roaming local bookstores, I notice a growing multitude of business books. Why write another? What makes this book different is that it looks solely to the book of Proverbs for business principles. I have written it for young businessmen and women everywhere, with the hope that they will become dedicated stewards who follow Christ with everything they have (Matthew 19:21; Mark 10:21; Luke 18:22).

Although written more than 2,700 years ago, Proverbs is just as relevant today as when the scrolls first absorbed ink from the end of a stylus. I think you will be astonished, as I was, at its relevance to any business environment, regardless of culture or economic situation. Its wisdom applies in any setting, country, time period, business, or ministry.

Proverbs contains a treasure trove of practical wisdom for all aspects of business. I don't want to waste that treasure. Others can write creative theories or procedural books for operating a successful business; I prefer to engage the young businessperson's heart through practical examples and stories about my application of the powerful truths found in Proverbs.

The book of Proverbs is God's inspired work, written primarily by Solomon, son of David, king of Israel. Solomon was the son of Bathsheba, who had an adulterous affair with David. God granted wisdom to Solomon so he could understand and obey God's law established through Moses (1 Kings 3:9,12).

Solomon's three thousand proverbs demonstrate the wisdom God granted him in answer to his desire to serve God as a shepherd of Israel. In spite of his wisdom, Solomon's fallen nature and excessive power led to choices that resulted in his decline to despair. Nevertheless, the content of the truth God gave him stands firm to this day, instructing us in righteous living.

In the prologue (Proverbs 1:1-6), Solomon states his purpose in writing. He says that proverbs are for obtaining wisdom, insight, discipline, prudence, knowledge, and discretion and for doing what is right, just, and fair. They help us seek, do, and develop certain things with the ultimate goal of becoming a wise and righteous person.

In a first reading through Proverbs, you may find it hard to grasp all the directives, commands, encouragements, and advice. Instead of following a clear theme, they wander in various directions, sometimes seeming to contradict each other. It is difficult to wrestle through this whirlwind of instruction and organize it in logical fashion. As I studied the book of Proverbs over a three-year period, looking for major principles with a view toward business application, I identified two themes: God's promises and our responsibilities in light of those promises.

1. God promises that he will:
   - Bless
   - Protect
   - Provide
   - Thwart

2. Our responsibilities are to:
   - Seek after these things
   - Do these things

- Develop these things
- Avoid these things
- Become these things

If we recognize the value of knowing God's heart, we will want to know what he loves and what he condemns. Because of our sin nature, our natural inclination is not to align ourselves with God's principles, but his Spirit convicts us when we veer from his path. Proverbs is an excellent road map for realignment as it instructs, encourages, and addresses so many different issues. The repetition of truths in various ways adds richness and intrigue to what might otherwise be a simple instructional manual.

If we fulfill our responsibilities of **seeking**, **doing**, **developing**, and **becoming** the things God loves and **avoiding** the things he condemns, we will stay on the path of righteousness. This path leads to a life that pleases God, and we experience his blessings and protection by aligning with his design for the business steward.

So, I encourage you to put this book to the test. I have endeavored to handle these holy truths and not add my own speculation. I have attempted to write clearly so that the Holy Spirit might convict each reader's heart regarding God's wonderful promises as elaborated in Proverbs. Alongside this book, I invite you to read the book of Proverbs and see for yourself how the Lord will reveal things to you as he has to me. I am confident you will be blessed as you seek these truths for yourself and apply what you find.

CHAPTER 2

GOD'S PROMISES

The overstuffed chair in which I sat, the plush decor of the conference room where I waited to be summoned back into the mediation—all of it presented an ironic contrast to the storm that collapsed the roof and ruined everything inside. Another irony: The images imprinted on my mind stirred deep empathy for our client in spite of my forced appearance as a defendant. I didn't want to be here. I struggled against being overtaken by fear, forcing myself to repeat Proverbs 3:5-6: *"Trust in the LORD with all your heart and lean not on your own understanding; in all your ways submit to him, and he will make your paths straight."*

I have a view of what I think God's blessing and protection should look like, and sometimes it doesn't match his view. Sometimes God's view is so different that I can't recognize it until much later. The lawsuit was an example. I prayed countless times to be delivered from it. I wanted a summary dismissal based on the overpowering evidence exonerating us. I wanted to avoid months of preparation and worry.

But the certified letter naming our firm as DEFENDANT set me on an unanticipated quest to protect both the firm and our reputation. Satisfied that we had adequately designed the roof drainage system to withstand a hurricane's onslaught, and that the contractor had not built the roof according to our drawings, I was faced with a strategic challenge: How could we establish our innocence without appearing to be simply avoiding liability? When everyone cries "Not guilty!" even the innocent can look suspicious.

I took comfort in conversations I had had with our client several months before. They weren't upset with us, nor had they understood we were being sued by their insurance unit. Nevertheless, whatever sympathy they may have had for our predicament, it wasn't their responsibility to dismiss us from the joint lawsuit against every potentially culpable party. Their insurer was merely pursuing the normal course of business with the expectation that the legal system would sort it out.

As we waited for the mediation to continue, my partner Shade O'Quinn and I discussed every nuance of the meetings up to that point, every stray remark that might offer a clue for adjusting our response. Normally, we would expect our attorney to handle this task with expertise beyond anything we could bring to the table. Unfortunately, the attorney our insurance company assigned to us in this mediation was not experienced in construction law. He had represented insurance companies for suits involving car accidents, but major construction projects were new territory to him. We found ourselves coaching him as he sat silent during most of the mediation.

"Okay," I said, looking up from my notepad. "It seems clear we have no risk of being found at fault for the roof collapse. I don't know why they waited until today to tell us about the independent engineering study; they pretty much took us off the hook. The downside is that it could still take a lot of time and money in the court system to prove it, and the contractor isn't ready to throw in the towel."

"Right," Shade said. "It's a huge relief to know the insurance company isn't coming after us for the whole loss. Now that it's limited to just their deductible instead of millions, it's a different ball game. Two hundred fifty thousand dollars is a manageable amount."

"All of us flew here just for the day," I said. "Nobody wants to miss their plane home or stay overnight. Even their insurance attorney wants to get this over with. Did you hear her mention she'd like to get back home for her daughter's soccer game tonight? She doesn't mind who's technically to blame for the roof collapse, she just wants her client to recover their $250,000 deductible, and I don't blame her."

We sat in silence for a minute while I tried to connect some dots. "Shade, what do you think of this idea? We could propose a settlement that would satisfy the insurance company without taking the whole responsibility on ourselves. Suppose we offer $100,000 and suggest that the contractor do the same."

"But it was their fault," Shade said. "Why should we pay any of it?"

"I'd rather not," I said. "But it could easily cost us that much just to go through full litigation, to say nothing of possible appeals. With all the evidence in our favor, this won't jeopardize our reputation. We'd be offering to go beyond what the law requires in an effort to contribute to a quick and reasonable settlement. And that's what they want, not a lawsuit."

We decided to extend the offer, hoping the contractor would match it. At first, he continued blaming us, but when his insurance company saw our willingness to negotiate with everyone's interests in mind—knowing we were not technically at fault—they began to sing to our tune. Four hours later, the contractor ended his holdout and we settled.

"I really appreciate the approach you took today," our client's attorney told Shade and me at the conclusion. "Can't say I've ever seen anything quite like it. About halfway through this thing I would have laid odds we'd go home tonight ready to file the papers to go to court. You guys maintained integrity."

"Thank you," I said, uncomfortable taking the credit when I realized God had given me the wisdom to offer up this settlement rather than hold fast to our innocence. Fishing for the right words, I finally responded with a smile and a handshake.

She smiled. "My company will get my full report on this, of course. Including my appreciation for what you have done today with their welfare in mind."

Everyone—even the contractor—left realizing it was a fair solution to settle out of court for amounts far lower than originally sought. As an unintended consequence of our mediation hearing, years of future work with this client followed us—along with significant income. Think of it: This incredible blessing was disguised as a serious problem in the form of a threatening certified letter. I love God's flair for the dramatic. I especially love it in hindsight.

WHAT GOD SAYS HE WILL DO

As a tapestry is woven with beautiful threads, God's promises are woven throughout Proverbs. These promises can be hard to understand, just as the nature of God can be hard to comprehend. Although we tend to connect promises with obligation, I didn't find anything in Proverbs that puts God under obligation; nor can I obligate him to comply with my understanding of his Word. We cannot simply name and claim God's promises for our own benefit. They are his promises that he will faithfully and conditionally bestow based on his desires and not our own. Who can fully comprehend the nature of God? Who can take him to court? We try our best to understand his promises, but all we can actually do is faithfully obey what we know will please him. This is the beginning of wisdom.

Nevertheless, God says he *will* do certain things. He will:

- Bless
- Protect
- Provide
- Thwart

For those who submit to his leadership, God offers wonderful blessings, protections, and provisions, as enumerated throughout the thirty-one chapters of Proverbs. He has also promised to thwart the efforts of wicked people who do not submit to his rule of order.

GOD'S GENEROUS BLESSING

If there is one thing I am sure of, it is this: God has richly blessed our business. Over the past thirty years he has provided a significant amount of profitable work throughout the United States, and I can find no better explanation than he chose to bless our firm for his own purposes. We don't deserve it, and the recession of recent years argues against any natural cause. We are clearly recipients of his sovereign goodness.

My business partners and I recognize that God has entrusted us with this business so that we may fulfill his greater purposes. Scripture tells us he wants us to use resources to take care of those who are on his heart. He doesn't bless us solely for our own consumption or benefit, but so that we might be vessels to funnel his blessings to others. After we support our employees' families, we use the remaining profits as God directs. His plan results in a divine chain of blessings, and he holds us accountable for our part in the chain. The blessings of God are not only for the righteous, but for those around the righteous (Proverbs 11:11).

I have come to understand that righteousness means living the right way before God. In other words, I must get to know and understand God's principles and obediently apply them to my life. Righteousness is also the application of God's truth to actions. I cannot live as a righteous man apart from an intimate, growing knowledge of God. I must be engaged with him through prayer and the study of his written Word. I must then listen carefully to his quiet, still voice. I must obey without hesitation, even before I have full understanding; sometimes obedience is the only path to understanding. Obedience develops personal discipline that results in a righteous lifestyle.

Solomon instructs those with wealth to give generously to those in need. The poor are mentioned over thirty times in Proverbs. The poor are those who cannot take care of themselves or generate income for their own care, including widows, orphans, foreigners, prisoners, and those who are disadvantaged, unrepresented, helpless, defenseless, enslaved, vulnerable, abused, and downtrodden. We will one day stand before Christ to give an accounting for the assets he has entrusted to our care. We know that *"from everyone who has been given much, much will be demanded"* (Luke 12:48).

Consider these verses that describe God's blessings:

- God blesses the righteous, and this blessing may bring wealth without *painful* toil (Proverbs 10:22).
- God's blessing is also in the form of wisdom, prudence, knowledge, and discretion (1:2-4).
- *"Good people obtain favor from the LORD"* (12:2).
- God blesses and prospers those who trust in him (13:21; 16:20).

- When our ways are pleasing to God, he causes our enemies to make peace with us (16:7).
- With God's blessing, there comes a future hope (23:18; 24:14).
- *"A faithful person will be richly blessed"* (28:20).

It appears to me that to receive God's blessing on a business, we must seek after him, trust his counsel in our decision making, and be obedient in the plans he reveals to us. We will be blessed when we are kind to the needy, reflecting the kindness and generosity God has shown us in spite of our inability to repay him.

GOD'S HAND OF PROTECTION

I can cite numerous instances of God's specific protection of our firm, even though I can't explain it. It may sound mystical to some and coincidental to others, but I don't need to be convinced; I was there. Although we do not physically see God, we can sense his presence not only through others who advocate for us but also in circumstances that unfold in front of us. Just as God is a mystery, his protection can be mysterious as well. The realm God works in is as invisible to our limited sight as wind or gravity or radio waves, but we don't deny their presence.

How many times have we cried out for God's protection? We beg him to look out for us, keep us from harm, and give us safety. In the direst circumstances we tend to shout even louder. Why would we naturally do this unless God created us to sense his presence? So, although it is difficult to explain, God works faithfully to protect us in many instances. And as we are admonished in James 1:5-6, we must ask for wisdom without doubting. God wants us to ask in faith, believing he will protect us according to his will, which is wiser and more comprehensive than the limited understanding behind our request.

Here are some of God's promises of protection in the book of Proverbs:

- *"He is a shield to those whose walk is blameless"* (2:7). In a battle, we need a shield to help us maintain integrity.
- *"He guards the course of the just and protects the way of his faithful ones"* (2:8). While we walk through our business, our steps will not be hampered and we will not stumble.
- Our discretion will protect us, and he will give us understanding that will guard us. Wisdom saves us from the ways of wicked people and keeps us from sexual improprieties, enabling us to walk in ways that are good and keep to the paths of righteousness (2:11-22).
- He will protect us by guiding us in the way of wisdom so we may follow his paths (4:11-12).
- The wicked will be swept away, but the righteous will stand forever. We know that the righteous will not be uprooted and the wicked will not remain (10:25,30).
- *"The righteous person is rescued from trouble, and it falls on the wicked instead"* (11:8).
- Fear of the Lord turns us from snares that would encumber us and lead to death (14:27).

In the fierce battles that rage unseen, we need God's protective shield. Although the enemy accuses us, we remain blameless when we hide behind God's protection. Being blameless does not mean being perfect in any self-righteous sense; it means being covered by God's righteousness, hidden behind his shield. God blesses us when we choose not to step out from behind his shield and compromise with Satan's deceptions. Satan, on the other hand, constantly tries to lure us out for a clean shot.

When we trust in the Lord with all of our heart, not leaning on our own understanding, he will make our paths straight. In other words, he will guide and protect us. When God guides us, our steps will not be hampered and we will not stumble (3:5-6,23-26).

One of the primary ways God protects us is through the wisdom he grants when we strive to walk in his ways. Obedience to him protects us from all kinds of dangers—not so much because he miraculously intervenes but because he doesn't have to. Obedience sets us on a wise course.

I've seen this over and over again, but a few examples stand out in my mind, including the protection that came from listening to his still, small voice during the mediation hearing. Let me show you what I mean.

Protection During the Mediation Hearing

It was a stressful feeling sitting in a roomful of lawyers, each positioning for his or her client. There were lawyers on the client's side, lawyers for the general contractor, a mediating lawyer, and our own lawyer. It seemed that each party was posturing with a win-at-any-cost attitude. My partner and I were both nauseous at the potential ramifications if we were found to be at fault. We certainly didn't feel any "love" floating around the room. Situations like this tend to bring out the worst in people. We were shocked to hear the things said about our firm as the other parties fought for self-preservation. We were accused and felt abandoned, with little opportunity to defend ourselves.

During introductory remarks, the contractor's attorney presented his client as a blameless victim merely "following instructions." *Our* instructions! We felt ambushed but remained composed and did not counter the allegations. We didn't know how to respond, and our attorney didn't say a word.

But when our client's attorney told us that a report by an independent consulting engineer had actually exonerated us from liability, we went from feeling attacked and defenseless to feeling vindicated. We felt God's protection but wondered about his timing, not knowing yet how the rest of the day would play out. With the burden now squarely on the contractor, his attorney began posturing in earnest. At this point, the mediator sent us into separate rooms to consult our own attorneys.

Our choice to settle quickly and avoid going to court actually protected us from what could have been a long, painful civil trial. God protected our business even in the timing. If we had known about the report in advance, we would have been more likely to stubbornly dig in and force a day in court.

One day could have turned into weeks or months and a lot of money, as well as possible alienation of our major client. God protected us, our reputation, *and* our future business.

In the middle of severe storms, we always feel disoriented, helpless, and sometimes even abandoned. The wise choice is to endure, trusting that protection is there whether we see it yet or not. God's protection has more to do with his mercy and goodness than our own righteousness.

Another remarkable example of how obedience leads to God's protection occurred when we were audited.

Protection During Audits

Years ago, four different agencies requested an audit of our firm: the state tax office, a major client wanting to audit our invoicing to their company, another state agency inquiring about our professional registration submission, and the IRS. My first thoughts were, *What have we done wrong? Why is this happening all at once?* As was my custom, I asked God to give us his wisdom and protect us. We have always intended to operate with integrity, be honest in all our dealings, report as required, and never hide anything. But this didn't prevent a sick feeling from coming over me. We had never been audited before and had no idea what to expect—and suddenly we were facing four of them! Soul-searching time again: Was I operating this company with integrity, or was I merely saying the words? Actions speak louder than words, and I had to trust that our actions would prove our words.

We had endeavored to be righteous, but until the flashlight

shines deep into the soul of the company, the truth is hidden. No one wants to be audited, even if they have nothing to hide or fear. No one wants to be examined at the level we were going to be examined! My partners and I prayed, "Lord, go before us in such a way that we will be exonerated for any misunderstanding. May we have the opportunity to fix any mistakes we have made."

Filled with the feeling of being taken apart, we began our own deep examination of our operations so we could provide full transparency and all the documentation required for each audit. Knowing that full disclosure is the best policy, we sought to discover any mistakes and identify any inappropriate expenditures.

I worked hard to sort out my private thoughts of embarrassment, pride, arrogance, apprehension, and bewilderment. I learned quickly that although we may be well-intentioned, we can never have absolute integrity. It was a hard lesson to internalize, because my pride had never allowed me to admit that. But as it turned out, the auditors did not find significant problems with our business returns. God had indeed answered our prayers for protection. Several of the auditors even complimented our accounting staff for their excellent documentation. Nevertheless, I was humbled by the incredibly thorough examination that went deep into the heart of our company's integrity. God's protection is there for that reason, to protect us when we are defenseless and vulnerable. He protects us according to his plan, in spite of ourselves.

And here's a third example of how obedience to God's ways leads to protection.

Protection When a Lawsuit Threatened

The telephone rang. One of our clients had a question, and the tension in his voice was evident. "We've got a problem. This building you designed has suddenly got a bunch of ugly cracks in the floor, and I need to know how serious it is. Is this thing going to fall down?"

There is no way to answer a question like that without an on-site evaluation, so my partner flew out immediately to inspect the project site.

"The cracks are ugly, all right," he said, "but there is no eminent danger of failure or collapse."

Somewhat relieved but unconvinced that the problem wasn't more serious, the client retained a local engineer to evaluate the severity. He reported to the client that the building *was* in eminent danger, ready to collapse at any time. Panicked, the client immediately shut down business and evacuated the building.

Our phone rang again. "My engineer says this thing could go down any time. I can't keep people in there after what he said. If something happened, it would be on my head!"

We immediately returned to the site for further evaluation. Confident that our design was adequate, we wanted to discover the cause of the cracking. But more important at the moment was proving whether the structure itself was as stable as we had earlier determined. Losses mounted with every day the business remained closed.

The first step was to physically test the slab to ensure its structural stability. The next three days were filled with extensive load testing, far beyond the slab's original design requirements. It performed without problem. Our relieved client reopened for business.

Still concerned about the cause of the cracking, we examined all the test evidence. The conclusion was that the contractor had not placed the reinforcing steel within the slab in the proper location, resulting in cracks around several of the building's columns.

What could have ended with a catastrophic lawsuit for our company ended in our firm being exonerated and our reputation protected. Although we used wise counsel and responded quickly, we saw God's protection throughout the process. We had asked him to reveal an approach to the problem that would accomplish two things: protect our client from loss and preserve our reputation as competent, thorough architects. The slightest innuendo can damage the perception of professionalism, and this can have two negative effects, regardless of actual performance: difficulty attracting clients and undermining a client's confidence, which may influence a client to make a bad decision.

In this case, closing the store was a hasty decision based on poor information. It resulted in losses that, if continued, would have been catastrophic for the client. To the degree that an extended closing happened because of a client's lack of confidence in us, we would bear some responsibility. Fortunately, this was not the case. The client did not pursue us for the closing of the store once they realized our design was sound. I sensed God's protection over our reputation and from serious financial loss.

God has promised that those who walk blamelessly will be kept safe, which gives great comfort and confidence to those in business (Proverbs 28:18). Walking blamelessly does not necessarily mean walking perfectly; we are all sinful and incapable of blameless living. It's an issue of the heart. Our *intent* is to walk blamelessly and please God, to seek his counsel and apply his principles to the best of our knowledge. Our blamelessness is a result of trusting in God rather than trusting solely in our own performance. We have an Advocate who protects us.

GOD'S MULTIFACETED PROVISION

Aspects of God's provision are enumerated throughout the Proverbs. Here is a sample selection:

- He shows favor to those who are humble (3:34).
- The Lord does not allow the righteous to go hungry (10:3); they will flourish with prosperity and be richly blessed.
- God's blessing (provision) brings wealth without *painful* toil (10:22).
- *"The house of the righteous contains great treasure"* (15:6). As I have been faithful in my intent to follow God, he has richly rewarded me by entrusting some of his treasure to my care.

God's provision is multifaceted, applying to both our spiritual and physical needs.

Provision of Spiritual Needs

Throughout the book of Proverbs we see God's provision of wisdom, discipline, understanding, insight, prudence, and discretion.

In the confusion and darkness I faced in our firm's ordeals, I desperately needed God's provision of wisdom. I was so grateful that wisdom doesn't need to originate in me and that I could count on the promise in James 1:5 that God would grant me wisdom. Although we develop our intellect, wisdom is understanding God's perspective on his world. God is the author of wisdom, and he delights in providing it to those whom he chooses. In fact, Ecclesiastes 2:26 tells us, *"To the person who pleases him, God gives wisdom, knowledge and happiness, but to the sinner he gives the task of gathering and storing up wealth to hand it over to the one who pleases God."*

One way God provides wisdom is through his loving discipline. It may not be comfortable at first, but the results of discipline are as beneficial as an athlete's workouts. Discipline can lead to understanding, insight, and discretion, and it can aid us in becoming godly.

God also provides counsel from three sources: his Word, other people, and from the Great Counselor himself, the Holy Spirit. We encounter this Counselor through his quiet voice in our conscience; his counsel is always consistent with his written Word.

God's spiritual provision allows us to experience fulfillment and live with contentment, a quality of life no amount of money can buy.

Provision of Physical Needs

God has provided our firm with wonderful work through our clients over the years. This provision for our physical needs has allowed us to build a strong business and take good care of our family of employees.

In the early years of our business, I was able to procure twenty or so architectural projects per year. This work resulted in a nice income for my family. As the years progressed, I began to see God's hand of provision through an increased number of clients and projects. I can't explain how I was able to obtain this additional work except to say it was provided through the generosity and goodness of God.

I didn't know where to look for this work, in spite of being attentive and pursuing leads and opportunities. Our projects came from referrals, contacts, and some of the most unlikely people; our success is the result of God's goodness. Our efforts were rewarded with much more new business than seems natural. I have always contended that the Lord did our business development for us. I could never have imagined how some clients would materialize.

For example, in 1990, I received a telephone call from a physician. Dr. Tom insisted I was the architect for whom he had received a referral — an architect named Harris whose father was a physician. He wanted to commission an ambulatory surgery center for his office, and I fit the description of the person he was looking for. I later learned I was not the Harris he had been referred to, but I ended up with the commission.

Tom and I met on numerous occasions and developed a close working relationship, which evolved into a dear friendship. His ambulatory surgery center, our first, was an efficient design that allowed him to perform procedures within his existing medical office. It was a relatively simple project but had complicated requirements due to licensure policies. The project rendered many subsequent referrals, driving us to become experts in small ambulatory surgery centers.

Another time, God provided work for us through a contractor. Our firm has been blessed to have the world's largest architectural client, Walmart. Let me assure you, my efforts at marketing had nothing to do with this. The only reason we have this wonderful client is because of God's gracious provision. All I had to do was respond to a simple request.

I was visiting with a contractor one day, and he asked if I could provide drawings to build a small addition to a Walmart store. Only a year into my practice, I was young and hungry and willing to provide service to anyone with a need. "Sure, I'll be glad to draw up a plan. How soon do you want it?" I replied, knowing it was a small job that wouldn't pay much. Another architectural firm had already rejected the job because "they didn't want to do this kind of work." Actually, it was because of their referral that I met Randy in the first place.

"Right away," he said.

I went to work on it immediately and produced the construction drawings he needed. Randy completed the project to Walmart's satisfaction, and we were all happy. I hoped I might hear from Walmart again, but it didn't happen.

One day the contractor called back. "Raymond, could you help me with another little Walmart project?"

I was, of course, delighted. That year I designed five small additions for Randy to construct. They all went well, and again we were all happy. But then something different happened. Walmart made a comment to Randy that would change my life: "Hey, tell Raymond he should give us a call sometime. We might have some other work for him."

That referral and the subsequent calls were not a coincidence. They were God's provision to eventually provide work for hundreds of employees for over twenty-five years. And it's not over yet; our work with Walmart continues.

Everyone can see the irony in a start-up architect backing into this incredible business because the big firm in town rejected it. Eyes of faith can also see that God provided that business seed and aided its growth into a tree, then an entire orchard. Yes, I did my part. I cultivated, watered, and fertilized, but God provided the miracle of growth. And I got to pick the fruit.

Just as a loving father provides for his children, so God provides for us. As the giver of good gifts, he lovingly gives us all things for our enjoyment (James 1:17). His provision is not a measured response equal to our goodness and efforts; it comes from his gracious heart as a good Father wanting to bestow good things upon us. His giving is pure because his character is pure. He will not be manipulated by expectations, claims, or demands, most of which come from a selfish attitude of entitlement. We have a God who provides.

Sometimes his provision comes in the form of thwarting.

GOD THWARTS EVIL PEOPLE

I don't recall ever hearing anyone teach on the idea of thwarting, nor have I read anything on the subject. So I was reluctant and a little intimidated to address the issue of God's opposition to certain people. Proverbs, however, says in numerous places that God thwarts or opposes wicked or evil people. Consider these verses:

- He opposes those who lie, devise wicked schemes, and stir up conflict (6:16-19).
- He impedes the progress of the cruel, perverse, and wicked (11:17-21).
- He thwarts perverse hearts (11:20; 17:20) and those who exploit the helpless or unprotected (22:22-23).
- *"The Righteous One takes note of the house of the wicked and brings the wicked to ruin"* (21:12).

Throughout Proverbs, wicked or evil people are warned of God's anger toward them. They are given to violence, bloodshed, and every kind of evil behavior. Because they harm God's creation in direct opposition to his nature, he hates their activities with a burning wrath.

God warns us to stay away from evil people at all costs, even to the extent of not crossing paths with them. He gives us the ability to do this through some provisions we've already described. He says, for instance, that discretion and wisdom will protect you (Proverbs 2:11; 4:6). *"Wisdom will save you from the ways of wicked men"* (2:12). God grants us wisdom and discernment to recognize and avoid circumstances that will put us in jeopardy to the schemes of wicked people.

Many of us have experienced an instinctive distrust of people who have later turned out to be evil. Sometimes their wickedness is apparent, because we can see their unethical or illegal activities. Other times, however, these activities are disguised to avoid detection. God, however, can see their hearts and will protect us from their schemes when we are seeking to follow his ways. He has certainly done this for me.

When I was first starting my business, I received a call from a developer who said he was building housing for older people in his community. I'm not sure how he got my name, but he knew of my expertise in designing assisted-living centers for the elderly. Catholic charities were backing him, and it sounded like an attractive program with philanthropic value.

I flew to his community to meet him and to see the project location and review its requirements. Already possessing a measure of discretion and wisdom that God was building in me, I felt a little discomfort during this first meeting. His office occupied the back of a used-car dealership and looked like it had been furnished by Goodwill. Dirty, disorganized, and with no decor other than calendars and posters, it was nothing like the offices of project developers and philanthropically minded people I knew. I withheld judgment, thinking this might merely represent a lack of concern with appearances.

He drove me to the site, and I was in for another surprise. The property looked more like swampland than a setting that could be developed to house older people. I still wanted to give him the benefit of the doubt, but his grandiose talk and spotty knowledge of development were making it more difficult.

On the flight home I weighed what I had seen and heard. Nothing conclusive, just some discomfort. Not wanting to misjudge a diamond in the rough, I decided to take a step at a time and send him a contract.

He didn't sign the contract, but he was in a big hurry for me to start working on the project. Because it's generally imprudent to invest much time in a project without a contract, I requested a retainer and did some preliminary work to help him commence the project.

He didn't send a check or respond directly to my request, but he did call and express anger that I wasn't prioritizing his project. As time passed without any reasonable action on his part, I finally withdrew my services, explaining that I didn't think he was operating in good faith. He again was angry and accusatory, but I didn't hear back from him. Less than a year later, I read in the paper that he was arrested and indicted for embezzlement, fraud, and murder. Finally exposed as a con artist, he had taken money from Catholic charities and spent it on unlawful activities, including the suspected murder of an associate.

I believe God thwarted the evil efforts of this man, and as a result he ended up in prison. I could easily have been entangled with him in business, possibly losing more than just my time and services. I had experienced a check in my spirit that led me to disassociate from him, ultimately keeping him from harming me and my practice.

Later, another phone call came, this time from a Florida developer also interested in providing housing for older people. Another nonexecuted contract accompanied by urgent demands for us to commence work. We provided some preliminary work and billed him immediately. You'll never guess; he didn't pay. But he did demand that we continue working. Funding was always just around the corner.

You might think you know where this is heading, and you would be right, but these guys always sound convincing. If they didn't, they would never get anywhere. What is obvious in hindsight is rarely clear as it is unfolding. That is why God's gifts of wisdom and discernment are so valuable. They again gave me a check in my spirit that we should cease working on this project unless the firm was compensated for our services. We stopped. The developer became angry and even threatened to sue us, although he had no admissible grounds.

In both scenarios, we were dealing with men who lied, who were proud and arrogant, crafty, perverse, and preying on the vulnerable elderly. I firmly believe God opposed these men and protected us from them.

Now that we have examined what God promises to do for businessmen and women who operate according to God's economy, I'd like to share what Proverbs has to say about our responsibilities in light of those promises.

CHAPTER 3

SEEK THESE THINGS

Treasures

As a scoutmaster for over thirteen years, I became fascinated with the older Boy Scout handbooks. In fact, I collected every published edition. My most valuable handbook is one published in 1910 by Lord Robert Baden-Powell, the founder of scouting. This particular handbook cost a lot of money, and my copy is in excellent condition. Because it means so much to me, I keep it carefully displayed in my glass bookcase so that it will be protected.

I also dabble in collecting fine art. I am most fond of one particular artist, and I have collected a number of his pieces. He has won several major museum shows and, not being a prolific painter, his art is rapidly increasing in value. Several of my favorite paintings by this artist are well known. I treasure them because of the quality of painting and the subject matter. I take very good care of these treasures, prominently displaying them for friends who come into my home.

The book of Proverbs identifies several treasures worth seeking earnestly, and this is the kind of care I believe we should give them. These treasures are particularly important for young men and women in business. Not easily obtained, they are to be esteemed, pursued, and cared for as priorities of our stewardship.

We are commanded above all else to guard our heart, because that is where we store our treasures. When our heart is filled with treasures mined from God's Word, we develop a heart of righteousness. Just as we store important things in our house to guard them from thieves, we guard our heart to keep the enemy from deceiving us and robbing or contaminating the treasures of truth we've stored there.

The treasures we are commended to mine are of great value in God's eternal economy. We are to seek:

- Wisdom
- Counsel
- Love and faithfulness
- Good reputation
- Righteousness

Let's look more closely at each of these.

SEEK WISDOM:
THE MOST VALUABLE THING ON EARTH

When I was a young man in college, I asked God to give me wisdom. Sometimes I would become impatient because I didn't see wisdom coming quickly. But I soon realized that wisdom is granted with time, and that I needed to continually ask God for it. Wisdom is developed through life's experiences and through the study and application of God's Word.

James 3:13-17 describes two kinds of wisdom. The wisdom from above *"is first of all pure; then peace-loving, considerate, submissive, full of mercy and good fruit, impartial and sincere"* (verse 17). This wisdom operates within God's economy, with attributes God loves. The world's "wisdom," however, is unspiritual, demonic, full of envy, selfish ambition, disorder, and every evil practice. This "wisdom" operates in the world's economy, with attributes God hates. The wisdom Solomon describes throughout the Proverbs is from above, the wisdom God wants us to seek and treasure.

It is important for young people in business to seek after wisdom just as they would build a suitable foundation for a building. The quality of the foundation's construction determines how a building performs over time. With the proper foundation, the building is stable and sustainable. Similarly, the foundation of God's wisdom will support the structure of any business; without it, the business will not be sustainable in God's economy.

According to Proverbs, nothing is worth more than wisdom: not gold, silver, or precious stones (3:13-15). We are to turn our car toward wisdom and seek it as hidden treasure. There is such a repeated emphasis on the value of wisdom that I have become convinced it must be the world's most underestimated treasure, worthy of a lifetime of pursuit.

Wisdom benefits a seeker by bringing peace, prosperity, honor, and long life (3:2,16; 8:18). If the price of wisdom is everything you have, make the trade gladly; seek it, get it, esteem it, and embrace it more than any other valuable thing.

Wisdom is sweet to your soul and gives you a future hope (24:14). A person without hope is a pitiful sight, and with storms always looming in the financial markets, those who trust in the world's economy are placing their hope in an unstable foundation. God's economy, however, has been designed with eternity in mind, and it is always hope filled. The people I know who operate in accordance with God's principles are hopeful, because they are always looking forward to eternity.

Wisdom is supreme. In fact, the Lord brought wisdom forth as the first of his works. He appointed Wisdom from eternity, from the beginning, before the world began. Wisdom was there when the heavens were set in place, before the clouds were established or the sea had its boundary. Wisdom was the craftsman at the Lord's side, delighting in humankind (8:22-31).

God uses wisdom to communicate with his stewards and direct them in the use of his heavenly treasures. Wisdom sees things from God's perspective, sees history past and looks into the hopeful future. Wisdom teaches us how to live skillfully in this world and prepares us to live in eternity.

The entire eighth chapter of Proverbs is written from the viewpoint of wisdom calling out to us. In verse 18, wisdom says, *"With me are riches and honor, enduring wealth and prosperity."* God gives wealth to the wise. I have come to understand that those who attain wisdom understand God's design for money. Because money, like every other resource, belongs to God, it is to be managed for his glory within his economy. For this reason, he looks for wise men and women to become his stewards.

Wisdom:

- Protects us from evil people
- Keeps us on the path with good and righteous men and women
- Prolongs our life
- Rewards us with prosperity so that our personal treasury becomes full
- Is far greater than gold or silver or precious metals
- Far exceeds any gem mined on earth
- Carries with it a future hope without end

Would you like these things in your life? If so, seek wisdom with all your heart; *"the one who gets wisdom loves life"* (Proverbs 19:8).

How do you seek wisdom as though it is treasure? The first step is to ask God for it. He has promised to give it as part of his provision.

Twenty-five years ago I was seeking to provide professional

services to a potential client. "Sorry, but my company doesn't have any work to assign at this time," he said.

I was disappointed, of course, but before I had time to think of a response, the words came tumbling out: "Well, I'm not interested in work at the moment, but I was hoping you might consider me for future work—maybe next year when you are allocating projects."

In retrospect I realize God gave me the wisdom I needed to respond in the moment; it was exactly what the client needed to hear. Not only did the company give us work the next year, they became a regular client with over twenty-five years of continuing work.

Wisdom's close companion is discernment. Both wisdom and discernment help us make right judgments about people. God gave me wisdom ten years ago in selecting employees who would eventually become my partners. Sitting in my office one day, the Lord planted this thought: *Call Shade O'Quinn and offer him a job. He needs a hand, and you need help.*

Shade had his own architectural firm, but it was struggling because several clients had not paid him. At the same time God was planting the thought in my mind, Shade was praying that God would deliver him out of his situation. He later told me he had asked God "to give him a shovel and just show him where to dig," and that he would be obedient to whatever God wanted him to do. The timing was perfect. Shade shut down his practice, moved his employee and furniture into our office, and became part of our firm. As we benefited from his hard work, integrity, and professional skills, the wisdom of God's prompting became clear. Five years after he joined the firm, we began working through a transition that resulted in Shade owning a significant portion of the company.

Wisdom often comes through a soft, gentle whisper from the Lord. I don't claim to hear God's voice often, nor am I always sure that what I am thinking is truly God's wisdom. But when I act in faith, responding to what I think is his wisdom, it usually turns out to be the case. God, as the ultimate good Father, is always happy to give his children wisdom when they ask for it. He delights in giving it, because he wants us to live righteously within his economy.

SEEK COUNSEL: COLLECTIVE WISDOM

Counsel is collective wisdom from others. People who seek advice are wise because they tap into a much greater reservoir of collective wisdom than they could bring to their situation on their own.

Proverbs says this about collective wisdom:

- Victory is won through many advisers (11:14).
- The wise listen to advice (12:15).
- *"Walk with the wise and become wise"* (13:20).
- *"Plans fail for lack of counsel, but with many advisers they succeed"* (15:22).

According to Proverbs, there are three places to obtain counsel: the book of Proverbs (along with other portions of the Bible), wise people, and the Lord himself.

The Book of Proverbs

By studying Proverbs (along with other portions of Scripture), we obtain counsel and instruction from God. The Proverbs guide us, so we will go on our way in safety and not stumble (3:23).

Wise People

Wise people, the second source of wisdom, can give *"heartfelt advice"* (Proverbs 27:9) and sharpen us as *"iron sharpens iron"* (27:17). My counselors love, correct, and rebuke me so I may become a sharper man. If I do not seek their sharpening counsel, I may miss something. I may be heading in a dangerous direction without realizing it. Their counsel helps keep me on track, sharpened and accountable.

My business partners are a particularly valuable source of wisdom. Because they know me well, I especially value their input before making any important business decision. This team approach has enabled us all to grow closer as we carefully consider our collective advice and measure it against the principles in God's Word.

As the sole owner early in my business, I didn't have the privilege of gathering collective wisdom from within the firm on difficult issues. Although I had employees, they were not the right people to consult regarding certain tough issues. It wasn't until our firm grew and our leadership developed and matured that I could tap this resource. Nevertheless, I knew I couldn't sustain the firm — or myself — without good counsel regarding projects, employment issues, and client concerns.

Fortunately, God supplied the people I needed. The greatest thing about my partnership with Larry Craighead and Shade O'Quinn is the collective wisdom they provide from inside the firm. We seek each other's counsel on a continual basis and find it extremely valuable in making the judgments necessary to sustain our firm. I certainly couldn't manage a large firm without it.

When we are in the habit of getting good counsel, it prepares us to be wise counselors for others. Collective wisdom goes both directions. As I have sought the wise counsel of my partners, I have noticed they reciprocate by seeking mine in their decision making. We have truly developed a "pleasantness of friends."

My greatest counsel comes from my wife, Marydel. God has given her insights into my business that defy explanation, but no one knows me better than she does. As my wife, she is part of me, and I would be denying God's design if I did not consult her. I am convinced God uses her to help me become a wiser businessman.

When difficult issues arise in our business, we sometimes go to the best outside counsel available. We generally consult other godly people for advice. Sometimes we need technical information; this comes from professionals, some of whom may not be Christians. We look for the highest level of expertise we can find in accountants, lawyers, and professional engineers. They don't make our decisions for us, but they give us data and context for applying our God-given discernment to important decisions.

I have found our best counselors to be those who are both experienced and humble enough to listen to all the facts. Prior to our roof collapse mediation hearing, we knew we needed legal counsel and professional engineering counsel to help us ascertain the facts surrounding the situation. We carefully selected the most knowledgeable, reputable engineer we could find. We were committed to discovering the truth, because we firmly believe we can usually handle the truth if we know what it is.

I've seen what happens to people who don't seek counsel. Left to their own wisdom, they miss the benefit of an alternative perspective and fail to recognize a blind spot or weakness. I recall withdrawing our professional services from one client because he wasn't taking our counsel. He had some ideas that were inadequate, clearly not in his own best interest, but he wasn't open to constructive input. His narrow-mindedness resulted in mistakes in construction methodology and even inappropriate placing of whole buildings.

Fortunately, he learned from mistakes and opened up to receiving counsel. We reengaged with his project several years later, and it was amazing what collective wisdom accomplished in building an effective project.

I've also observed people who ask for counsel but don't listen to the advice they're given. They usually struggle with hidden pride that they may not recognize. Humility has taught me to always listen to counsel and evaluate it against the truth in God's Word. We who are entrepreneurial leaders must be especially aware of the pitfall of stubbornness.

True humility leads to the best safety net I have found: listening to counsel.

The wisest people I have observed in life are those who take and apply advice (Proverbs 13:10). Those who respect commands will be rewarded, according to Proverbs 13:13, and those who heed instruction gain understanding (15:32). Those who walk with the wise become wise (13:20). As the old saying goes, "You become like the company you keep."

The third place we find counsel is from the Lord.

The Lord

It has been my practice to go to the Lord for his counsel prior to undertaking any serious task. Sometimes he responds in the quietness of my heart. Sometimes he leads me to a passage in his Word that speaks to my concern. Sometimes he leads me to godly people who have the experience to clarify the situation.

No wisdom, insight, or plan can succeed against the Lord (Proverbs 21:30). If we commit to him whatever we do, our plans will succeed. Although we plan a course in our heart, the Lord determines our steps; all our steps are established by the Lord (16:9).

I endeavor to use all three sources of counsel to ensure I am gaining the full benefit of God's provision: consulting his Word, developing relationships with wise people, and maintaining an intimate relationship with the Creator of business.

SEEK LOVE AND FAITHFULNESS:
WRITE THEM ON YOUR HEART

Love isn't typically discussed in business books, nor is it something taught in the business world. But we know that the greatest commandment is to love God and love our neighbors (Matthew 22:37-39). *"Let love and faithfulness never leave you,"* Solomon said to his son. *"Bind them around your neck, write them on the tablet of your heart"* (Proverbs 3:3). Those who plan what is good will find love and faithfulness (14:22). As the apostle Paul said in 1 Corinthians 13, we can do incredible things, including giving away all our possessions and even sacrificing ourselves, but if we do them without love, they don't profit us anything. Christ said the greatest thing we can do for our brothers and sisters is to love them. Paul reaffirmed this by saying that of the three qualities that remain—faith, hope, and love—the greatest is love (1 Corinthians 13:13).

For the first ten years of my company, I strove to be an excellent architect. I studied hard in school to become a professional capable of producing excellent designs. I worked diligently and pulled many all-nighters. But ten years into my practice, something changed. The Lord began giving me the desire to become a good employer, a desire that seemed to override my desire to become a great architect. God, working deep in my heart, was developing my love for the people around me. I can neither explain it nor take credit for it, but he was changing a high priority for a higher one. I had wanted to become a great design architect; he wanted me to love people and become a great employer. The desire to become a great employer led me to encourage my employees, enabling them to sense my care.

My attempts to be a good employer were clumsy at first. In my desire to get hard work and excellence from my employees, I was hard on them and lacking in compassion. Recognizing this wasn't having the desired effect, I began to pray for my employees and their well-being. I kept a list and prayed for each employee by name, asking God to grant him or her success at work. This led me to be more compassionate regarding their personal lives. My desire for their success began to transcend my concern for their performance in the firm.

Slowly I came to the conclusion that what was best for them would actually be best for our company. I began to look at things from their perspective to see if there was anything I could do to help them be more successful in their personal and professional lives. I was beginning to look out for their interests even more than my own.

I'm not suggesting that my motivation was totally altruistic. I made all kinds of mistakes, but my growing concern for the welfare of our people actually resulted in our firm growing in size. It seemed that God was entrusting more people to my care as an employer. As our firm grew, our professionalism continued and our profitability remained. This was inexplicable, and I sat back in amazement as I watched God work in my own life to make me more compassionate.

I have told interviewees that I really loved the people who worked here and I thought this would be a great place for them to work as well. I mean that, but it isn't always easy.

I sometimes become upset with the attitudes of our staff, and it is hard work to look at things from their perspective and love them regardless of how they act. But this is what God calls us to. When we seek love and faithfulness, it changes our heart attitude — and it changes the attitudes of those we seek to love.

Many conflicts with people abate when they know they are loved. As an employer, my demonstration of love and concern is shown in how I treat my employees and in my attitude toward them. What better description of love can there be than 1 Corinthians 13? When these characteristics are applied in our business dealings, it's amazing how conflicts diminish. Love and its partner, faithfulness, were so important to Solomon that he instructed his son to write them on the tablet of his heart.

My most valuable employees are those who are faithful even when not being supervised. Their faithfulness is epitomized by Proverbs 27:18: *"The one who guards a fig tree will eat its fruit, and whoever protects their master will be honored."* If my employees take good care of our company, they will benefit from the "fruit," or profit, the company yields. I will also honor faithful employees because they help make the company great. When I find a trustworthy employee, it refreshes my spirit (25:13).

I think Solomon brought love and faithfulness to his son's attention because they are foundational to God's eternal economy. If I endorse a culture of love and faithfulness within our business, I stimulate everyone to have the freedom to excel.

With this encouragement, our employees seem to work harder, appreciate their employment more, and experience less strife within the office environment.

Although competitive by nature, most employees don't enter into office politics if the threat of condemnation and discouragement is removed. When employees see that their managers care for them, they have a great sense of security and freedom to achieve their goals. The attitudes of love and faithfulness help motivate employees, ease conflicts, and align with God's purposes for business.

He who covers an offense promotes love because *"love covers over all wrongs"* (Proverbs 10:12). *"Through love and faithfulness sin is atoned for"* (16:6). These verses foreshadow the demonstration of God's wonderful love through the sacrificial life and death of Jesus Christ. This Love walked on earth, exemplifying the greatest business command of all. We too are to love those around us and serve through faithfulness.

SEEK A GOOD NAME: REPUTATION

"A good name is more desirable than great riches; to be esteemed is better than silver or gold" (Proverbs 22:1). More important than skill and talent, a good reputation serves businesspeople far beyond their ability to continually develop new customers. Here's a case in point.

In 1992, I received a phone call that knocked me out of my chair. Without warning, a large corporate client was firing us.

"I hate to tell you this," he said, "but you need to stop

working on all of our projects now and send all the information to another firm we're working with."

"This comes as quite a shock," I said. "I wasn't aware of any problem. What have we done?"

"I know it doesn't seem fair," he said, "but it has nothing to do with you or your work. In fact, you've provided the highest-quality work for the lowest fees we've ever enjoyed. I'm afraid it's all about politics."

I felt a hole in the pit of my stomach. What kind of strategy can you develop for influencing the office politics of a huge corporation in another state? Feeling somewhat helpless, I was reduced to the hope that our reputation would later rescue us from this unfortunate event. And it did.

The corporation's own staff architects and real estate managers immediately came to our aid. Over the next two years a myriad of various departments contracted with us for architectural services. Ironic as it may seem, the other architectural firm failed in its duties, and we later received back most of the work that had been taken from us. A good reputation, it seems, can even overcome politics.

In working with clients, I've noticed they tend to be more concerned with confidence in the quality of our firm and our people than in the specific services we provide. This has led me to the theory that what our clients perceive is just as important as the actual service. I've gone so far as to tell our staff that our client's perception of our service is even more important than our service; but I hasten to add that if we don't back up the perception with great service, we won't keep the client.

In the beginning of a relationship, perception based on our reputation is all we have, and it is enough. But if our work results in disappointment, our reputation cannot prevent their perception from being damaged; they'll fire us. When clients lose confidence, it is hard to rebuild. If we tell a client we will meet a deadline and then miss it, the client will have difficulty trusting us to meet future deadlines. We could meet every subsequent deadline for a long time before changing their perception that we are always late. This has happened to our staff, and we have seen how future contracts can go to others as a result.

Any business that provides goods or services faces the same threat. If promises are broken, it builds a perception that is very difficult to overcome. No wonder Proverbs is so adamant about protecting our reputation! Because an offended party is so difficult to win over again, it's much easier to maintain a good reputation than to repair a damaged one.

Clearly, our reputation for diligence is more valuable than any advertising we could buy. In fact, our firm has not had an active marketing campaign during its thirty-year tenure, relying instead on our professional reputation for repeat business.

Our firm's reputation is built around service, and one of the ways to keep clients for years and years is by emphasizing service. Keeping clients is the most important part of the success equation of a business. As a business leader, I must serve our employees in a way that enables them to take great care of our clients. Although design is certainly very important in our business, clients desire relational service more than avant-garde design.

Once a reputation is damaged, it's like letting out a secret that cannot be called back. Have you ever sent an e-mail you later wished you could recall? Better to guard your reputation and protect it. Treat it as something very valuable and fragile. For, as King Solomon advised his son, a good reputation is worth far more than gold and silver.

SEEK RIGHTEOUSNESS: BE BOLD AS A LION

The righteousness described in Proverbs should be the overall goal of the young businessperson.

Proverbs says this about righteousness:

- We are blessed if we seek after righteousness because the Lord will protect and provide for the righteous (2:7-8; 3:33).
- The righteous walk securely, are never uprooted, and stand firm forever (10:9,25,30; 12:3).
- The Lord guides the righteous and rescues them from trouble (11:3,8).
- The pursuits of the righteous reap a sure reward just as the desires of the righteous end in good (11:18,23).
- *"The house of the righteous contains great treasure"* (15:6).
- The Lord loves those who pursue righteousness, and he hears their prayers (15:8-9,29).
- The righteous man's children are blessed after him (20:7).

What great affirmations from God himself, that he loves us as we pursue righteousness and listens to us as we pray. This is a great encouragement for the young business leader.

So, what do righteous men and women look like? The righteous embody the qualities God desires in his people: good, appropriate, and wise in both attitude and action. Their actions help them escape trouble and avoid the schemes of evil and wicked people. Seeking to exemplify God's own character, they love and serve their neighbors. They are after God's heart and want to please him. They fear the Lord and live rightly before him. They become students of the Bible and obey God's commandments and principles as they understand them. Obedience without hesitation leads them to deeper understanding and an intimate relationship with God. Righteousness is a high priority, so they seek it and mine it from the pages of Scripture.

The righteous will leave an inheritance not only for their children but also for their grandchildren (13:22). This conveys the idea of passing on part of God's abundance to bless future generations, but we know that sometimes an inheritance can become a curse. Insecurity may cause people to fearfully hoard wealth, not releasing it until they no longer have a choice. Many businesspeople store their wealth and leave an overabundance for future generations who are unprepared to handle it. This results in a double loss: the good that could have been done and wasn't, followed by the self-destruction of incapable beneficiaries when the benefactor is no longer around to help.

I believe wealth should be stewarded to future generations

appropriately, which includes ensuring that beneficiaries have the training and wisdom to handle it. Large amounts of money can have negative effects on children and grandchildren who have not learned to be stewards. We know from Proverbs that an inheritance claimed too soon is not blessed (20:21).

I have elected to distribute my children's inheritance to them as younger adults while I can help them manage the assets. My hope is to benefit them early in their lives when they might have a greater need than when they are older.

When the righteous prosper, those around them rejoice and prosper. The blessing is distributed outward like a rising tide lifts the ships around it. Unfortunately, this blessing doesn't occur in many poor third-world countries where the wealthy do not bless those around them and actually hoard or consume their wealth without sharing. It is all the more remarkable when the benevolence of the wealthy righteous blesses the community around them. God is certainly the greatest example of this benevolence as he shares his creation and abundance with those who follow his principles.

In our firm, we strive to live by this principle in sharing our abundance with our employees. God's blessing of profitability has enabled us to bless our employees through large bonuses, good benefits, and a generous attitude toward them (Proverbs 21:26). We recognize that our entire team contributes to our prosperity, and we desire to see all of them share in the blessing. However, we don't want to overcompensate or unnecessarily reward those who don't earn their portion. Neither do we want to ruin our employees as an inappropriate inheritance might ruin a child. But prosperity, properly distributed through a generous employer, can do wonders for the morale and encouragement of the staff.

Proverbs also tells us that the righteous are cautious in friendships (12:26). This is particularly important in forming partnerships that can affect your reputation. Proper alignment with those who enter into business and financial relationships with you can prevent much heartache.

I began my business without partners. In fact, I was careful not to have partners for the first twenty-five years of my career because of this principle. I was already married to the most important partner of my life, Marydel. She has always been a great partner in my business as well as my most important adviser. To me, a partnership is a joining together that is not easily separated. I have seen many business partnerships destroyed because of the casual nature of their beginnings; they should never be entered into lightly.

I had the desire to establish a business without the encumbrances or concerns of a partnership. As the business grew, however, I felt the need to have additional burden-bearing capabilities that could come only through a true partnership. Because I knew that selecting partners of integrity is paramount—affecting both our ability to perform and our reputation—I chose people who exemplified integrity and righteousness in their actions. I saw these qualities in them firsthand. This kind of cautiousness in friendships, particularly in financial matters and partnerships, is another benefit of living by God's wisdom and economy.

"*Whoever pursues righteousness and love finds life, prosperity and honor*" (Proverbs 21:21). Recognize the deception that says financial success is the only success in business. Pursue instead the success exemplified by true life, God-given prosperity, and eternal honor.

What man would not want this on his tombstone:

He lived an outstanding life.
He was prosperous in God's economy.
He is honored in heaven.

Those who pursue righteousness will find these things, but the price of righteousness is a life dedicated to humbly seeking God's wisdom through mining Scripture and carefully obeying its direction. Righteousness seems to be the bottom of the funnel of all the godly characteristics displayed in Proverbs.

Just as we spend great energy mining gold from deep within the earth, we must spend great energy mining the treasures of wisdom, counsel, love and faithfulness, a good reputation, and righteousness. This is not merely a list, but a treasure chest that will help the young business leader discover a life of success in God's economy. When these treasures become deeply rooted within our heart, we learn to live the righteous life that helps us function successfully.

CHAPTER 4

DO THESE THINGS

Disciplines

Final building inspections tend to raise my blood pressure a notch, especially when the inspection involves a surgery center and the Department of Health. This particular day, however, was a dream: Everything was as it should be, and the inspector seemed almost . . . friendly.

"I'm really impressed," he said, "with the way you've organized this surgery center into such a small space."

"Thank you," I said, smiling at my client, the owner-doctor who was along for the big event. "That was an important criterion for the doctor, and I think it brought out the best in our team."

The inspector scrutinized the last room, scribbled a few more notes in his book, and walked with us to the front door. We said our good-byes, and I was just closing the door when he turned like Columbo, halfway through the door, and said,

"Oh, I just thought of one more thing. What type of fuel system are you using for the emergency generator?"

"Natural gas," I answered, "because the system is on the roof."

He shuffled back through the door and said, "Well, that's a problem. We don't allow natural gas, because it's an unreliable fuel source for emergency generators."

My blood pressure went up a notch. The facility was scheduled to open shortly, and the Department of Health license was critical to our deadline. Switching out the generator system would take months, not to mention extra cost. Fighting panic, I responded simply and quietly, "There is nothing in the regulations that prohibits this type of fuel system."

"Doesn't matter," he said. "In my opinion it's unreliable. Unless you provide other evidence of redundancy in the emergency systems, I'll require a diesel-powered generator."

I knew from experience that diesel generators could not be refueled on the roof. Natural gas was the only type of system allowed for a rooftop-mounted generator. The doctor was in shock. He stood petrified and speechless until the inspector left. Then, exhibiting the same kind of forced control I had just used, he turned to me and said, "I don't want explanations and I don't want excuses. I just want it fixed."

Let the scramble begin. Back at the office, not knowing how to solve this problem, I asked God for wisdom. Then I recalled the inspector's use of the words "other evidence of redundancy." *There's got to be a way,* I thought, *a way to use other systems— not to provide primary emergency power but to augment it.*

We came up with a plan. Add additional batteries for the lights, alarm systems, emergency call systems, and anesthesia. The air conditioning, not considered critical for licensure, could continue to be powered by the emergency generator without additional backup. We took the further step of classifying the emergency generator as the secondary emergency backup, using the batteries as our primary backup system. The state thought the idea was excellent and approved the facility within a week. This experience confirmed to me the value of trusting God.

In Proverbs we are told to follow four commands. These four commands are like disciplines leading to a righteous life that pleases God:

- Trust in the Lord.
- Honor the Lord.
- Do what is right.
- Guard your heart.

These four simple commands are repeated throughout the Bible. Early in Israel's history, Moses instructed the children of Israel to live by them, and later the Ten Commandments reinforced them. God's law requires all to honor him; honor is implicit in the first commandment, to love the Lord with all your heart. The Ten Commandments are all about trusting the Lord to define what is right. Some of them help us guard our heart by avoiding idols or anything that threatens God's priority in our life. Throughout their history, Israel was constantly coming back to God, renewing their trust in him to deliver them not only from their enemies but also from their own sinful disobedience.

The Old Testament prophets were required to do what was right at the expense of their own comfort and security. Daniel risked his life to do what he knew was right when he stood up to Nebuchadnezzar. Many prophets were killed for doing the right thing and saying what God told them to say. Idol worship, in particular, was a constant theme because its result was the same as today: entangling, enslaving, and drawing people deeper into detestable practices and away from loving and serving God.

Let me share with you what I have learned as I've done my best to put these four commands into practice so I might run my business in accordance with God's economy.

TRUST IN THE LORD WITH ALL YOUR HEART

I remember driving to the office one day not long after I started my company, wondering how I would get my next project. Beginning a new firm as a young man trying to support a family is a difficult challenge. Knowing I had no work to do, I asked the Lord for guidance. I remember putting my trust in him, confident that he would always provide for me.

I had barely settled into the chair at my desk when the phone rang. As you've probably guessed, my next project was on the other end of the line. I remember that instance so well because of my acute desperation, my choice to trust in the Lord for provision, and his trustworthiness "just in time."

All businessmen and women can relate to having the need to trust in God. Because of our sinful nature, each of us has a fear of insufficiency. Our sufficiency and confidence come only when we trust in the Lord, just as Solomon instructed:

- *"Trust in the Lord with all your heart and lean not on your own understanding; in all your ways submit to him, and he will make your paths straight"* (Proverbs 3:5-6).
- *"Commit to the Lord whatever you do, and he will establish your plans"* (16:3).
- Pay attention to the Proverbs: *"So that your trust may be in the Lord, I teach you today"* (22:19).
- *"Those who trust in the Lord will prosper. Those who trust in themselves are fools"* (28:25-26).
- We need not fall prey to the snares of fearfulness when the Lord is our confidence. It is quite an assurance to know that *"whoever trusts in the Lord is kept safe"* (29:25).

We know it is impossible to please God unless we trust in him. *"Without faith it is impossible to please God, because anyone who comes to him must believe that he exists and that he rewards those who earnestly seek him"* (Hebrews 11:6). This is by God's design, developing our faith in him rather than in our own prideful self-sufficiency. Our greatest trust seems to arise out of relying on him in the midst of a crisis. I am most eager to cry out to the Lord when I realize I am insufficient to solve a pressing problem.

A young businessperson is wise to trust God for everything he or she needs to be successful. As we saw in chapter 2, we can trust in God's provision, we can trust in God's blessing, we can trust in God's protection, and we can trust that God will thwart those who threaten him. We are blessed to have a God who listens and answers us as we trust in him. He is always trustworthy!

Trusting in the Lord is part of our faith journey. Knowing that without faith it is impossible to please God, we exercise our faith by trusting in him. As with any discipline, exercise is a crucial component.

As a young businessman, I exercised my trust in the Lord in most situations. I trusted him to be my business development partner to help me sustain my business with appropriate work. I trusted him to bring the right employees at the right time so that I could accomplish the work. I trusted him to protect me from evil people and unjust circumstances. I trusted him to give me wisdom and skill to operate prudently and effectively. There was no part of my business that didn't require trusting in him.

If I hadn't developed that trust, I would have resorted to leaning on my own understanding, and that would have led me down a crooked path rather than the straight one God provides when you submit to him *"in all your ways"* (Proverbs 3:5-6). His straight path of righteousness enables us to be effective within his economy and kingdom.

HONOR THE LORD WITH THE FIRSTFRUITS

I can honor the Lord with my lips, but there is no better way to honor him than from my heart. It is undeniable; a person's heart is tied to his or her money. Money is the great motivator of most businesspeople, and when we honor God with it, we demonstrate trust and worship him with our heart in a most intimate way.

We are told, *"Honor the LORD with your wealth, with the firstfruits of all your [labor]; then your barns will be filled to overflowing"* (Proverbs 3:9-10). This is abundance! I recognize that God has given me the ability to generate profits, and I have endeavored to honor him with the "firstfruits" of our company's profits. At the end of each year, after the bills are paid and bonuses are distributed to employees, the remaining profits are distributed to my partners and me. When I take my portion of the profits, I honor God by worshipping him with the firstfruits — the profits. My first act is to honor him, returning what is already his.

Marydel and I realize that everything we have has been granted to us by the Lord because of his generosity and love. These blessings are entrusted to us so that we may take care of them and steward them into his kingdom. The profits I receive from our business are for the purpose of taking care of my family and sharing with others in need.

Everything I receive serves a purpose greater than just my personal consumption or pleasure; God is training me to be a trustworthy servant and manager of his assets. For me, honoring the Lord with the firstfruits means listening carefully and distributing the profits where he directs. His direction typically comes through a quiet voice, confirmed by Marydel's agreement. When the Lord speaks to us, we believe it is important that we distribute the profit quickly in order to honor him. Honoring the Lord through giving of the firstfruits gives us a great sense of peace, joy, and contentment.

One of the most effective ways we can honor God is by sharing our wealth with those in need. Helping the less fortunate is an extension of our worship. It is my conviction that just as the righteous bless all those around them because they prosper, generous businesspeople were created by God to bless others (Proverbs 11:11; 29:2). After all, God has generously blessed us, and we should pass these blessings on to others.

Honoring the Lord with our wealth is only one component of honoring him. Obedience is the greatest way to honor the Lord; it is the action that shows our faith to be real. Obedience in all things is a great challenge, but Marydel and I are witnesses of God's generosity to us as we live according to his encouragements, warnings, and commands.

I must remember that my provision is always the result of God's blessing; there is no other enduring source. My appropriate response to this provision is to honor him, acknowledging his blessing by living righteously. Heeding his warnings, receiving motivation through his encouragements, and obeying his commands lead me to worship him through giving generously.

DO WHAT IS RIGHT

Several years ago, our company faced a dilemma. My senior management team had become complacent, and our work ethic was sliding into mediocrity. The diligence that once represented our firm was waning, and it was noticeable to our clients. Morale was at a low point and our managers were unmotivated to take the necessary corrective actions. I determined our biggest problem was the example they were setting. Leadership is best demonstrated through action, and we were not getting diligent, hardworking effort from these managers. Doing just enough to look busy, their individual performances sagged until the whole team suffered.

I made the hard decision to fire five managers on the same day. I knew it was risky, and I had to be sure my decision was right. Once I was certain this was the necessary and best solution, I had to execute it. It was painful for them and their families. It was unpleasant for me because of things that would later be said about me. Knowing I was justified in terminating them, I had to do the right thing.

The results were undeniable. The next year our profit nearly doubled, office morale strengthened, and our clients complimented our increased quality. The decision had been hard, but it was the right decision.

Doing the right thing is at times messy, difficult, unpopular, politically incorrect, and even hurtful in the short term. The benefits, however, are always the same: alignment with God's purposes and long-term good. Although I find nothing harder in my business than doing the "right" thing all the time,

I am convinced that it is not a mere option for the successful businessman and woman. The consequences of ignoring this simple precept are too devastating. It may be difficult, but doing the right thing becomes a matter of obedience; there is no good option but to execute it and allow the results to fall where they may.

One of the most common questions is, how do I know the right thing? It takes God-given wisdom (Proverbs 2:6) to know and do the right thing, and his Word is our primary source for wisdom. Without the wisdom found in God's Word, we make judgments based only on our own perceptions, often faulty assumptions that lead to logical but wrong conclusions. *"There is a way that appears to be right, but in the end it leads to death"* (16:25). Obeying God's Word aligns us with his will, his kingdom, and his economy. Unfortunately, many business and employment decisions are not clearly defined by a scriptural example. Knowing God's Word well enough to understand the principles and apply them doesn't come easily. It requires saturating ourselves in the Word, meditating on its meaning and asking for wisdom to understand the principles. Casual, quick reading of Scripture does not drive it down into the heart and soul.

Right thinking leads to right doing. The more our heart is saturated with God's Word, the more his principles become part of our automatic, conscious processing, changing the way we look at problems. Solutions quickly suggest themselves when the principles of God's Word filter out the confusion of our limited human perspective, and we make better decisions.

I urge you to learn this early rather than through the school of tragic experience.

When we saturate ourselves in God's Word, we develop a sense of discernment in dealing with people. This has been an effective tool that God has used to help me lead our firm's personnel. Intuition helps when there is no clear example to follow or when a serious event requires an immediate decision. I can't describe exactly how intuition developed in my own life, but it seemed to surface when I asked the Lord for wisdom in dealing with personnel decisions, as in the example I gave earlier.

Doing the right thing often requires courage. We sometimes have to jump into the middle of unpleasant issues we would prefer to avoid. Most of us, if we are honest, avoid, procrastinate, or delegate difficult tasks. Instead, we must "bring our boots to work"; we must wade into the problem in order to solve it. Boots bolster courage by providing some protection from the nastiness of current conditions.

I have served on several not-for-profit boards and committees of volunteer organizations. While serving in this capacity it is sometimes difficult to do the right thing, particularly when you are not in agreement with other board or committee members. It's much easier to go along with the group. When I have a conviction about an issue, I muster the courage to stand up for what I feel is right, regardless of who agrees. I have found that when I stand according to my convictions, others who kept silent frequently agree and find the courage to follow. Don't get me wrong; I don't take pleasure in disagreeing. I find it uncomfortable, even embarrassing. But when I am convinced my conviction is not for personal gain and is really about doing the right thing, I seldom regret my actions. I find that bravery is a cumulative characteristic: Over time I have become braver as I have practiced doing the right thing.

We know that when we do the right thing, we are in alignment with God's desires, his kingdom, and his economy. We have confidence that doing *"what is right and just is more acceptable to the LORD than sacrifice"* (Proverbs 21:3). It's the Lord's high priority for us to execute righteousness and to be just in our dealings. He would prefer to see worship demonstrated through these actions rather than hear our religious praise.

GUARD YOUR HEART ABOVE ALL ELSE

There is hardly a more important commandment than to guard your heart; the quality of your relationship with God is at stake! That's why Solomon said, *"Above all else, guard your heart, for everything you do flows from it"* (Proverbs 4:23). He went on to say, *"Keep my commands in your heart"* (3:1). The heart is not only the source of our actions, but also the place commands are to be stored—along with the treasures we talked about in chapter 3. The immense value of our heart merits guarding it with all vigilance. *"Take hold of my words with all your heart"* (4:4).

Meditate on these verses:

- *"My son, do not forget my teaching, but keep my commands in your heart"* (3:1).

- *"Let love and faithfulness never leave you; bind them around your neck, write them on the tablet of your heart"* (3:3).
- *"Then he taught me, and he said to me, 'Take hold of my words with all your heart; keep my commands, and you will live'"* (4:4).
- *"My son, keep my words and store up my commands within you. Keep my commands and you will live; guard my teachings as the apple of your eye. Bind them on your fingers; write them on the tablet of your heart"* (7:1-3).

Clearly, the heart is the essence of a person, the deep spring from which the water of a person's soul flows. Protect it with fences that block contamination and corruption.

Guarding your heart against the things that negatively affect your business includes guarding your tongue, guarding against dangerous contaminants, and making yourself accountable.

Guarding Your Tongue

How much damage is caused by the tongue! How much havoc our speech can create! I think guarding our heart includes guarding our mouth (Proverbs 16:23). The mouth expresses thoughts deep within the heart. When James described the importance of guarding or controlling the tongue (James 3:2-8), he was emphasizing Solomon's point about guarding the mouth.

When we control our mouth in business, our words will not damage relationships with clients, customers, employees, and coworkers. Many proverbs talk about the tongue spewing out curses or speaking words of blessing. In the search for valuable disciplines, controlling what we say competes for a top spot.

I told the story in chapter 3 about the day our major client called and told us to stop work on all of their projects and transfer everything to another architectural firm. I remember thinking I needed to be careful what I said. After verifying that the change wasn't due to issues on our part, I immediately thought to thank this client for the valuable work they had provided for us in the past. In doing so, I was actually blessing my client.

"I've got to tell you, Raymond," he said, "I didn't expect to hear that. Every other time I've had to make a call like this, I've gotten a bunch of complaints. People get bent out of shape and take it out on me. And here you are expressing gratitude."

I couldn't have told you why I said what I did. I just felt prompted to say it. Of course I had feelings of anxiety and anger over being fired, but I sensed my expression of gratitude would serve our firm well in the future. By guarding my tongue, I was actually guarding my heart as well, not allowing resentment to grow, but replacing it with a sense of gratitude.

If you can guard your tongue, you will have great mastery of yourself. These strong statements from Proverbs are particularly important to remember when dealing with clients, customers, employees, and vendors in business:

- A man of knowledge uses his words with restraint and is even-tempered (17:27).

- *"Even fools are thought wise if they keep silent, and discerning if they hold their tongues"* (17:28).
- Those who answer before listening show their folly and shame (18:13).
- *"Those who guard their mouths and their tongues keep themselves from calamity"* (21:23).

I train all our employees to be careful in how they communicate with clients. Their speech has everything to do with our success. Gently answering an irate client can easily prevent anger and diffuse an otherwise volatile situation. Proverbs 15:1 states, *"A gentle answer turns away wrath."* I make sure everyone knows the telephone receiver must be down if they want to vent their frustration! It's okay to be upset, but controlling your tongue with others is crucial to prevent conflict from escalating into a chronic negative relationship.

The tongue can also be used for good:

- *"The lips of the righteous nourish many"* (10:21).
- *"Those who guard their lips preserve their lives"* (13:3).
- *"How good is a timely word!"* (15:23).
- *"The hearts of the wise make their mouths prudent, and their lips promote instruction"* (16:23).
- *"Gracious words are a honeycomb, sweet to the soul and healing to the bones"* (16:24).
- *"Like apples of gold in settings of silver is a word spoken in right circumstances"* (25:11, NASB).

- Speech can be used effectively to encourage and stimulate employees. A gentle tongue can even break a bone (25:15).

The Sundown Rule, one of Walmart's cultural rules, has become part of our company's culture because of its profound effect. The rule simply says to return all telephone calls before the end of the day (sundown). It truly exemplifies Proverbs 15:23: A timely word is good and shows respect for others.

We are warned to avoid people who talk too much, because with a multitude of words sin is unavoidable (10:19). The only way gossip, a primary sin of the tongue, can be avoided is by controlling speech. I've seen plenty of damage from gossip, but I have never once seen it be constructive or encouraging. It is toxic to both the gossiper and the "gossipee."

- *"Without wood a fire goes out; without a gossip a quarrel dies down"* (26:20).
- *"The words of a gossip are like choice morsels; they go down to the inmost parts"* (26:22).
- Those who drop a matter avoid a dispute. Those who cover an offense promote love (17:9,14).

Wise businesspeople have the discipline to keep themselves and their tongues under control. That's why it's so important to always put down the receiver if tempted to express your frustration!

Guarding Against Dangerous Contaminants

When I was sixteen years old, I changed the oil in my car one day. Being lazy, I simply took the used oil and dumped it out into a field adjacent to my house, pouring it into a hole without any thought of the consequences it could have. The next day I noticed the creek next to the house had a shiny film on top. The used oil had migrated from where I dumped it all the way to the creek in one day. I felt terrible knowing that this small amount of oil could cause a traveling oil slick, contaminating the creek. I never did that again!

The things that contaminate our heart start so small that they are easy to overlook or underestimate, yet they can grow to become deadly. The most dangerous contaminants are:

- Pride and arrogance
- Love of money and the desire to be successful in the world's eyes
- Inappropriate relationships that lead to sexual temptation
- The lust of power and the desire to be important

Contamination of the heart starts subtly with an attitude that goes unnoticed. I've had to deal with all of these contaminants at some point in my career. I've learned to recognize the symptoms and potential damage when I am tempted. I have learned to flee things I know are not pleasing to God. I can't flirt with temptations; I am foolish to think I can resist. We never grow old enough or mature enough to stop being tempted in these areas. I have found the best option is to simply run from things that could be disastrous. (We'll talk more specifically about avoiding dangerous attitudes and behaviors in chapter 6.)

Guarding Your Heart Through Accountability

There are areas in my business life I must be held accountable for in order to guard my heart. I am accountable to my partners for my behavior around other employees and for how I handle the firm's finances. I give accountability authority to those closest to me so that I handle the firm's money with financial integrity. This helps keep me honest by providing a barrier between untruthfulness and my heart.

I've learned that total integrity is an impossibility, a self-righteous deception that invites disaster. Because I am an imperfect man, I don't have the capability of maintaining 100 percent integrity. But God doesn't require perfection in human performance; he desires our heart to lean toward him, asking forgiveness for our shortcomings and seeking to follow him by trusting and obeying as best we can.

Although our actions can be a witness to those around us, they only reflect the condition of our heart, the "wellspring of life" where our treasures are stored. If God can capture our heart, he will have our actions as well. It is the only recipe for a long, obedient life of faith expressed in righteous living.

Businesspeople who want to be successful in God's economy must take these commands to heart: They must trust in the Lord, honor the Lord, do what is right, and guard their hearts.

Although these commands may seem simple on the surface, they are far from easy to master. Because our old nature is constantly at war with these commands, we need the diligent discipline of an athlete to implement them in running a business pleasing to God. Ask God to give you the discipline you'll need to put these commands into practice.

CHAPTER 5

DEVELOP THESE THINGS

Habits

I recall many mornings watching the sunrise from the east window of my office. It wasn't because I came in early; it was because I had been there all night. During the first year of my practice I had to work extremely hard to establish the firm. I am convinced that if I had not worked hard initially, I would never have developed the high standards of practice and professional quality of work that have supported long-term relationships with my clients. I never thought I could work so hard, but I don't regret it. My diligence and hard work have been rewarded with a large, well-established firm.

Hard work is one of the habits outlined in the book of Proverbs that matures us into righteous living and enables us to build and lead a successful business. In addition to hard work, Proverbs talks about the following behaviors and qualities:

- Discipline
- Integrity
- Generosity
- Financial prudence
- Employee development
- Planning
- Discernment and sound judgment

All these habits are crucial to becoming excellent leaders and effective stewards within God's kingdom.

DEVELOP HARD WORK: GOT PROFIT?

My stepdad made this profound statement: "The specter of starvation makes one work hard." He was actually summarizing Proverbs 16:26, *"The appetite of laborers works for them; their hunger drives them on."* Hard work and diligence go hand in hand.

What It Means to Work Hard

Because I saw the benefits of hard work, I established a culture of hard work within our firm. Everyone who works for us knows they must work extremely hard. Yet there is a big difference between working effectively and giving the *appearance* of work. Proverbs recognizes this and does not equate hard work with putting in a lot of hours. Hard work means efficiencies, not just long hours. Our firm's culture prizes focused effort with a goal of producing value. A great example of this efficiency occurred several years ago.

Our relatively young team was tasked with producing a large number of remodel projects for a major corporate retailer. Short of staff and unable to find enough qualified professionals, we had to work many long nights and weekends to stay on schedule. It became a high priority to produce teamwork efficiencies that would eliminate redundant work. We developed an incredible sense of camaraderie in the process. When one architect had to stay late for his project, often others would stay with him, not only encouraging him but moving the project along more quickly.

We completed our work within deadlines and earned the privilege of a significant amount of work the following year from the same client. During this time we didn't work unnecessary hours; we just learned to be efficient in how we produced our work, and the team bonded.

Working hard is sometimes related to the tenacity to push forward until a task is completely done. Because I have inspected many construction projects over the years, I can do it almost effortlessly. If I am not careful, however, overfamiliarity can lead to complacency, as it did with a project in Idaho.

Nearly done with a routine construction inspection, I was about to take a shortcut and call it a day. Just then a gust of wind took a page from my clipboard and blew it onto one of the lower roof portions of the new building. As much as I didn't want to have to find a ladder and climb up there, neither did I want to lose the information on that page and have to recreate it. Without joy, I climbed onto the roof and began searching for the paper. That's when I noticed it: a construction deficiency that was quite serious. The holes for the roof drains were not large enough to accommodate the anticipated drainage requirements. This could have led to a severe problem and potential collapse.

I thank God for the important lesson he taught me that day: Never become complacent or slack in your work; it can lead to a crisis. Slackness and complacency are enemies of a business. Those who are slack in their work actually destroy the business for which they work (Proverbs 18:9). Our company is careful to terminate those employees.

The Ant Versus the Sluggard

There are seasons for work in all businesses, times when strategically essential tasks must be done in order for profit to be possible. That's one reason why Proverbs uses the ant as an example of a diligent worker. The ant works hard at the appropriate time for his food and saves for the future (6:6-8; 30:25). In agriculture, there is an appropriate time to plant and to harvest. Sluggards (lazy workers) may be motivated at harvesttime, but their lack of motivation for plowing and planting leaves them with no crop. *"Sluggards do not plow in season; so at harvest time they look but find nothing"* (20:4). The lazy person is told not to love sleep but to get up and work. Oversleeping results in lost opportunities and poverty (6:9-11; 20:13).

Sluggards are also vulnerable to the deadly thief of craving (21:25). In other words, their poor work habits will eventually be their demise as their pursuit of pleasure and the easy life derails them from working hard in the proper season. Instant gratification has never been a greater temptation than in our advertising-driven, media-saturated culture.

Hard Work Leads to Abundance

Probably the most important verse I have applied in my business is *"All hard work brings a profit, but mere talk leads only to poverty"* (Proverbs 14:23). Just as diligence and hard work go hand in hand, there seems to be a correlation between diligence and prosperity.

Here are some of the principles that reflect this:

- *"Lazy hands make for poverty, but diligent hands bring wealth. He who gathers crops in summer is a prudent son, but he who sleeps during harvest is a disgraceful son"* (10:4-5).
- If you work hard in your business, you will have an abundance (12:11).
- The work of your hands will reward you (12:14).
- *"Diligent hands will rule, but laziness ends in forced labor"* (12:24).
- The diligent person works hard to obtain the possessions he prizes (12:27) while the lazy person disregards discipline and comes to poverty and shame (13:18).
- *"A sluggard's appetite is never filled, but the desires of the diligent are fully satisfied"* (13:4).

Those who work hard will have an abundance (12:11; 14:23). Those who simply chase fantasies will have a life filled with poverty or missed opportunities. The key is to work hard and smart (strategically) instead of simply dreaming or talking about it.

Work, although rewarding, is neither easy nor permanent. Nature—at least in our fallen world—is subject to decay and disorder. When we cease working the land, for instance, it naturally reverts to a wild, overgrown state not productive for human support. In placing us on the earth as its stewards, God has given us the work of subduing and replenishing it in a way that leads to order, community, and prosperity.

DEVELOP DISCIPLINE: A PREREQUISITE FOR SUCCESS

One of the surest routes to success is discipline. An unattractive path at first, when discipline becomes a habit, it surprises us with rewards. *"Whoever disregards discipline comes to poverty and shame, but whoever heeds correction is honored"* (Proverbs 13:18). Discipline is a prerequisite for becoming a prudent, honest, and diligent businessperson. Without it, these characteristics never develop into maturity.

If there is anything I learned from athletics, it is that discipline is required to achieve any level of success. When I was a young man, I dreamed of becoming a great wrestler. I soon discovered it was impossible to make progress without developing a disciplined lifestyle of physical conditioning and mental preparedness. Pursuing that dream set me on a path that prepared me for a greater dream. Today when I wrestle, it is with the problems of life and business. The self-discipline that became my habit early in life now serves me in a way I could never have imagined. Some tasks don't seem important enough to be worthy of diligent focus, but discipline leads me to do the best I can, an attitude that results in excellence in my profession.

I often receive documents for a last check before they go out to general contractors. It's tempting to skim over them because, quite frankly, thorough checking is tedious, time-consuming, hard work. I know, however, that mistakes find hiding places that keep them undetected in the absence of close scrutiny. I also know that mistakes lead to consequences during construction, and sometimes even years later. By disciplining myself to examine documents carefully, I avoid future problems.

Proverbs uses the word *discipline* in two different ways. The one we have been describing refers to training in order to develop desirable characteristics, the kind that will make us successful in God's economy. The second use of the word refers to rebuke or correction.

Consider how these two verses work together to show how we should give and receive corrective discipline: *"Stern discipline awaits anyone who leaves the path; the one who hates correction will die"* (15:10). *"Discipline your children, for in that there is hope; do not be a willing party to their death"* (19:18). Disciplined business leaders respond to the corrections and rebukes given in the Proverbs because they realize that *"the LORD disciplines those he loves, as a father the son he delights in"* (3:12). Because corrective discipline is essentially pain for a benefit, we are wise to welcome it.

Discipline also helps us develop restraint when temptations lure us. Those lacking it also lack judgment and end up paying the price.

- By exercising discipline, you can obey this command: *"Hold on to instruction, do not let it go; guard it well, for it is your life"* (4:13).
- Those who lack discipline come to the brink of utter ruin in front of others. *"For lack of discipline they will die, led astray by their own great folly"* (5:23).
- The undisciplined fall into many temptations by listening to the voice of folly. She leads them to *"the realm of the dead"* (9:18).
- *"Whoever heeds discipline shows the way to life, but whoever ignores correction leads others astray"* (10:17).
- *"Those who disregard discipline despise themselves"* (15:32).

DEVELOP INTEGRITY:
ACTIONS SPEAK LOUDER THAN WORDS

A company operated with complete integrity is hard to find. Most businesses proclaim their honesty, but it is conditional. Integrity demands complete honesty, even when no one will ever find out.

Proverbs says:

- *"Whoever walks in integrity walks securely"* (10:9).
- *"The integrity of the upright guides them"* (11:3).

- Honesty in speech is closely akin to honesty in actions. *"Kings detest wrongdoing, for a throne is established through righteousness. Kings take pleasure in honest lips; they value the one who speaks what is right"* (16:12-13).
- *"One whose heart is corrupt does not prosper; one whose tongue is perverse falls into trouble"* (17:20).

A wonderful example of integrity is found in something my business partner did before I met him. Shade O'Quinn operated a small architectural firm providing services to large churches. As ironic as it may seem, several churches did not honor their contracts and pay for services rendered. They didn't dispute their obligation; they merely refused to pay because they ran out of money.

This created a double problem for Shade, because he had subcontracted his engineering services. He lost not only his profit and wages but also the funds to pay his engineering consultants. This ultimately forced him to close his practice. Many people in that position would express regret to their consultants and walk away. Not Shade. He placed a second mortgage on his home so he could honor his agreement with his consultants and pay them everything he owed.

Shade demonstrated commitment to this truth: *"Better the poor whose walk is blameless than the rich whose ways are perverse"* (Proverbs 28:6). Situational ethics and convenient honesty may be acceptable in the world's economy, but God's economy is more durable. Within two years, Shade faithfully paid all his debt without ever receiving payment from his clients. He showed his faith through trusting in God's principles more than in his own security.

Many in that situation would have filed a lawsuit against the nonpaying churches. They would also have filed bankruptcy or refused to pay their consultants. If they subsequently won a settlement in a lawsuit, they would likely have kept the money for themselves, because the bankruptcy filing would have released them from paying their debts. Shade's integrity to pay others when he went unpaid is unusual in any profession and makes the world take notice.

Sometimes people get away with deceiving others — in rare exceptions for a long time — but the Lord is not deceived, and he detests it. The Lord detests differing weights and abhors dishonest scales, but accurate weights are his delight (11:1; 20:10,23). *"Honest scales and balances belong to the LORD"* (16:11). If you believe God *"exists and that he rewards those who earnestly seek him"* (Hebrews 11:6), would you want to engage in something he detests?

Honesty is as much a part of integrity as honest weights are in a transaction. This honesty applies through fairness with others, especially in fair pricing or negotiating an equitable transaction. Honesty goes deep into the core of a person's heart, and those who remain honest even when no one is looking exemplify the heart of integrity.

While bribery is not legal in the United States, its close cousins influence peddling and coercion are common and can be a temptation to businesspeople. Showing appreciation in the business world conveys a spirit of gratitude; however, financially influencing others in business can be a form of the dishonest scales mentioned in Proverbs.

We have to examine our heart to see if we have integrity in all aspects of our business dealings. I had to do this recently during an IRS audit. I had espoused running a business with integrity, and I endeavored to be honest in all my dealings. But several instances surfaced where I had, in fact, been dishonest with minor expenditures. I had forgotten about them, and they were brought to light almost ten years later during this audit. Although they were insignificant to the overall audit, what bothered me was that I had been less than honest in even the smallest of details.

I had purchased some artwork to hang in the office. Once these pieces were fully depreciated and no longer of value to the company, I knew we would replace them. When the time came, I decided to take them home. Although they no longer had any value on the firm's books, they certainly retained some residual value, yet I did not reimburse the company for them. This might be common practice, but I had a flippant attitude toward declaring a value and reimbursing the company for it.

The audit brought this to light, reminding me that although it had happened many years ago, I had not been completely honest. The auditor, incidentally, saw it as a minor issue and was not concerned about it, but it was of great concern to me because it violated a principle I strive to live by: *"Whoever can be trusted with very little can also be trusted with much, and whoever is dishonest with very little will also be dishonest with much"* (Luke 16:10).

DEVELOP GENEROSITY: ALWAYS BUY LUNCH

Proverbs has this to say about generosity:

- *"One person gives freely, yet gains even more; another withholds unduly, but comes to poverty"* (11:24).
- *"A generous person will prosper; whoever refreshes others will be refreshed"* (11:25).
- *"The righteous give without sparing"* (21:26).
- God blesses the generous (22:9).

The world's economy encourages us to pay only when absolutely necessary and to hold back when we can benefit from it. That's because generosity goes against our nature. It must be developed through the deliberate, continual practice of giving abundantly to others. That's one reason why when I go to the dry cleaners, I usually tell them to "keep the change." It does two things: It regularly reminds me to be a generous giver, and it also allows me to bless those who work hard on my behalf. Generosity simultaneously blesses others and strengthens a spirit of gratitude. Generosity often generates generosity.

Be Generous with Vendors and Service Providers

Paying our bills on time communicates a spirit of generosity and wins favor among vendors and consultants. When we are generous with vendors and service providers, we benefit because it blesses them and encourages them to deliver good service or quality workmanship.

Here's an example of how this works. One of our vendors, a faithful printer, has done work for our company for over twenty years. This printer has consistently provided excellent service, always showing gratitude for our business and cheerfully responding to problems. During a recent recession, knowing that their business was down, we sent them an extra check at Christmas. We considered this a bonus for the printer's efforts and faithfulness through the years, and we wanted to communicate our appreciation. They were astonished that we would make an unsolicited payment. Not only did it bless them, but they have continued to bless us with excellent service.

Be Generous with Employees and Business Partners

Throughout this book I have mentioned—and will keep mentioning—that because God has been generous with us, we want to extend the same attitude to everyone in our firm. This not only honors God, it also keeps us humble, because it is a reminder that our success comes from God and through the efforts of our employees and business partners.

One memorable example of generosity was the way my partners treated me following our ownership transition. When I sold a significant portion of the company to my partners, I was careful to be generous with them by offering a modest sale price. This decision made the transfer more affordable, giving my partners confidence that they could thrive. They recognized this generosity and worked hard to complete the transaction, following it with generosity of their own. Once the transition was completed, they voluntarily reimbursed me for the previously discounted value. This generosity meant more to me than they ever dreamed.

Another example of generosity occurred when several of our employees were nearing retirement age. They were in the position of many people today, looking forward to retirement but fearing they might have to delay it because of inadequate funding. Our firm elected to give them a large financial bonus prior to their retirement announcement. This enabled them to anticipate retiring comfortably on their time frame rather than having to stay longer for financial reasons. As a result, they were honored and blessed and gave great effort in their last years of employment.

Be Generous to Those in Need

Throughout Proverbs the wealthy are encouraged to financially aid the poor and protect the rights of the destitute (31:8). *"Blessed is the one who is kind to the needy"* (14:21). *"Whoever is kind to the needy honors God"* (14:31). *"Whoever is kind to the poor lends to the LORD, and he will reward them for what they have done"* (19:17). What greater goal for generosity than this? Generous people will be blessed themselves because they share with the poor. It appears to me that God always intends excess to be used to help those in need. This confidence led my wife and me to begin investing in charitable endeavors that directly affect the poor, the defenseless, and the illiterate. When we stand before the Lord one day to account for our stewardship, we will be asked, "What did you do with what was entrusted to you?"

DEVELOP FINANCIAL PRUDENCE: SAVE THE RUBBER BANDS

The financial business principles in Proverbs are profound:

- Spend less than you make (21:20).
- Pay bills on time (3:27-28).
- Be frugal (21:5,20).
- Avoid debt and surety (22:7; 6:1-5; 11:15; 17:18; 22:26).
- Save money, little by little (13:11).

Spend Less Than You Make

I have used this principle in business more than any other. Spending less than we make leads to accumulated wealth. With accumulated wealth, a business enjoys the freedom of options. *"There is desirable treasure, and oil in the dwelling of the wise, but a foolish man squanders it"* (Proverbs 21:20, NKJV).

Pay Bills on Time

Withholding or delaying payment for services or products can be easily justified. In God's economy, however, we should never withhold good from those who deserve it, especially when it is in our power to act (Proverbs 3:27-28). This means we should always pay our bills on time. Timely payment supports trust and loyalty in relationships, which contribute to prosperity. I feel this speaks louder than anything we could ever say to our vendors, and it earns us a favorable reputation.

Be Frugal

Our business endeavors to be frugal. It is certainly easier to reduce expenses than to generate more income. We keep overhead expenses to a minimum, reinforcing the idea of spending less than our income. For example, when our firm first opened, the budget for office supplies was very limited. The U.S. Postal Service provided a quality rubber band each morning around our bundled mail. By saving these rubber bands, we were able to go several years without buying any. This practice continued even after the company began to prosper and grow. It became so engrained in our staff that several assistants saved rubber bands for us even after they left the firm. Occasionally, I receive a bunch of rubber bands in the mail with a note.

This frugality led to the greater concept of prudence, especially in how we approach expenses. Although it may seem obsessive to save rubber bands, it fosters frugality in even the smallest of details. Small details will usually affect big projects; so we continue to save the rubber bands and paper clips, knowing that frugality leads to profit.

Avoid Debt and Surety

The greatest advice I received as a young businessman was to stay unencumbered by debt. Our firm started without debt and has operated since its inception without incurring debt. This has given us tremendous freedom and flexibility during difficult economic times.

Only one verse in Proverbs warns against taking on debt. Proverbs 22:7 says, *"The rich rule over the poor, and the borrower is slave to the lender."* Simply stated, when we borrow from others, we enter into obligation and bondage to them for our debt. Until the debt is satisfied, we have exchanged some of our freedoms for what we borrowed. Surety is closely aligned with debt, because it guarantees repayment of another person's borrowing. Debt and surety put both the borrower and the guarantor of surety in bondage. Current events in the world's financial markets illustrate the stresses that accompany entire nations when debt gets out of hand. The attraction of easy money obscures the hard payback.

God desires us to be free and unencumbered so we might focus on the important things of life. The pressure of repaying debt weighs heavily on our emotions, distracting us from serving fully in his kingdom. The pressure of debt is like the stress of carrying a heavy backpack: It's uncomfortable and keeps us from enjoying the journey. When it comes to your business, it's wise to keep your backpack as light as possible, avoiding heavy debt and long-term lease commitments.

Although there is only one verse in Proverbs about going into debt, there are many warnings against being surety for others. *"Whoever puts up security for a stranger will surely suffer, but whoever refuses to shake hands in pledge is safe"* (11:15). *"It's poor judgment to guarantee another person's debt or put up security for a friend"* (17:18, NLT). We should not put up security for others' debts, because the lender can take away not only what we've pledged but other assets as well if our collateral is inadequate. In an extreme case, we may also lose one of our most important assets, our reputation.

- Spare no effort to free yourself immediately if you become security for others (6:1-5).
- *"Whoever puts up security for a stranger will surely suffer"* (11:15).
- *"Take the garment of one who puts up security for a stranger; hold it in pledge if it is done for an outsider"* (20:16). In other words, it's a bad bet.
- Do not shake hands in a pledge or be security for another's debt (22:26-27).

Putting up security, or cosigning a loan, puts us in the same bondage as being in debt ourselves—with one big difference: We don't get the benefit of the asset for which the money was borrowed. Several years ago, I was tempted to become security (or surety) for my two business partners. During our ownership transition, we had the option of funding the transaction through borrowing money from our local bank. In order to securitize the loan, I would have had to personally guarantee my partners' portion of repayment by taking the loan proceeds and depositing them back in the bank as security. In the banking industry this is known as a "CD-backed loan." In the business world, this is the most desirable way to securitize an obligation.

I received counsel regarding this transaction and was told it was the safest strategy because it made repayment readily available. Regardless, I was concerned that it would violate the basic principle of not being surety for others. If my partners failed to repay their portion of the loan, the bank would ask me to turn over the cash to make the payment. I would not have been in bondage with this situation, but something about the transaction still bothered me. My intent with the ownership transition proceeds was to make other investments. Obligating the proceeds of the loan as collateral would restrict the funds and my freedom to invest in other opportunities, including charitable work. I was also relying on the stability of the bank to return my proceeds once the loan was paid. In recent years this is a concern due to bank failures in an uncertain economy. We elected not to fund the ownership transition through a bank loan. Instead, I loaned my partners the money personally, which did not violate this security principle.

Save Money, Little by Little

When we save money little by little, it has a tendency to grow (Proverbs 13:11). The simple act of putting aside even a little money on a regular basis results in dramatic growth with compound interest over time. Every investment has three components: basis (principal), length of time, and rate of return. The greatest of these components is the length of time the money is invested, making the amount not as important as the act of setting it aside and letting it grow.

DEVELOP YOUR EMPLOYEES: KNOW THE CONDITION OF YOUR FLOCKS

I've always tried to live by two adages: Take good care of your employees and they will take good care of your company, and what's best for the employee is best for us.

We need to be wise in our dealings with our most important asset: our employees. To be good employers we must know our people well and give careful attention to them, as good shepherds know the condition of their flocks (Proverbs 27:23). We should be familiar with each employee's talents, capabilities, and limitations. In addition to stimulating growth, bolstering strengths, and supporting weaknesses, we should encourage our employees when they do excellent work. This expresses loving care that leads to employee dedication and unconditional support.

In order to maximize efficiencies and profits, we must utilize our employees well, or a "low harvest" of their efforts will result. By placing our employees in their best position, we capitalize on their talents and ultimate job satisfaction. In contrast, some businesses, when they have positions to fill, immediately hire from outside rather than utilizing their current employees well. This generally leads to lagging productivity. Our firm endeavors to determine the talent of our staff and to place them in positions that will complement their strengths and abilities while they grow in skill. By understanding each employee and evaluating performance, we match the employee with an optimum job, resulting in a win-win situation for all. This is not only good for the company, it is good for the employee.

Several years ago we had an excellent intern architect working for our company. He excelled as a young professional while living with a burning desire to coach football. Although he worked diligently, his heart was unsettled with his professional vocation. After he'd been with us a couple of years, we encouraged him to pursue his dream of being a high school coach. He left and became an outstanding football coach. He is successful in his new vocation, and we are successful employers because we knew him well enough to perceive what was best for him and encourage him to do it, even though it meant losing an outstanding employee. Several years after he left the firm, he referred an outstanding architect to us. We subsequently hired that young man and gained the wonderful benefit of his expertise. In the end both employees and employer were blessed.

Sometimes employee development means correcting deficiencies. This correction is similar to pruning a tree. Pruning redirects growth for improvement, shape, and beauty. When done properly, it also adds to the tree's health. Pruning our employment tree maintains a healthy, vibrant, and growing staff. We prune through the discipline and, when necessary, termination of employees. Although painful at the time, the results are undeniable. As with the tree, the wounds heal, the tree is strengthened, and the fruit is better.

DEVELOP PLANNING: REMEMBER THE ANT

I have always taken planning seriously. While still in college I set goals and objectives, planning for my future as a professional. Years later, almost all of my goals had been accomplished. There seems to be something almost magic about putting goals in writing. Seeing the past benefits, I have continued to write goals and objectives for our business. By planning and seeking the Lord's wisdom, I am allowing God's purpose to prevail in my life and in the business.

Some people fear that planning and goal setting interfere with God's plan for their life. Quite the contrary is true; when we submit to him, he gives us the desires of our heart and stimulates our thinking to formulate our future according to his plan. Now that I have partners, we seek the Lord's wisdom while planning for our employees, clients, and profits. God always seems to honor the planning process within our firm as we commit our plans to him.

- *"Commit to the* LORD *whatever you do, and he will establish your plans"* (Proverbs 16:3).
- A person's steps are established by the Lord (16:9).
- *"Many are the plans in a person's heart, but it is the* LORD's *purpose that prevails"* (19:21).
- *"The plans of the diligent lead to profit"* (21:5).

Wise planning involves prioritizing our work in terms of both importance and sequence. Proverbs says to finish your outdoor work, get your fields ready, and then build your house (24:27). The following story illustrates the wisdom of this.

Dillard came to work for us with high expectations on his part and on ours. I considered him a good prospect for future management in the firm. Once on board, however, he focused on building his own home rather than developing business for the company. Buying a lot of things and designing an expensive house became such a distraction that his contribution to the firm suffered. Prioritizing his personal business over his employer's business proved to be a disaster. When recession affected our business and client base, his position was no longer needed.

Wise planning takes into account what will benefit and complement our effort rather than waste it. People in our profession tend to focus on producing current projects without prospecting for future work. This leads to a cycle of completing current work and then desperately looking for another contract. Procuring future work is a strategic activity that must be planned, scheduled, and protected to prevent loss of future income.

It is important in our planning to be careful not to boast about the future. The Lord gives us each day as a gift, and we do not know what it may bring forth. So when we are planning, we do it with hopeful optimism, committing our planning to the Lord and trusting him for a successful future.

DEVELOP DISCERNMENT AND SOUND JUDGMENT: A CLOSE CALL WITH REAL ESTATE

Solomon admonished his son to *"preserve sound judgment and discretion"* and not let them out of his sight. *"They will be life for you . . . and your foot will not stumble. . . . Have no fear of sudden disaster"* (Proverbs 3:21-23,25). This critical advice goes hand in hand with wisdom and prudence.

- Discerning hearts seek knowledge, and those who are wise in heart are called discerning. *"A discerning person keeps wisdom in view"* (17:24; see also 15:14; 16:21).

- *"The fear of the* LORD *is the beginning of wisdom, and knowledge of the Holy One is understanding"* (9:10). With this fear we will have sound judgment, insight, and power (8:14).
- Kings reign because of this judgment, and leaders make just decisions (8:14-16).

Discernment regarding people is a skill developed over time. It comes through experience and the exercise of sound judgment.

My wife exercises great discernment. Not long ago, I was considering investing in a residential real estate property that was part of a new development in an upscale suburb. I thought it was underpriced and ripe for an excellent return. Marydel thought differently, discerning problems on the horizon. I trust her sound judgment, so we didn't proceed. In time it became clear this would have been a poor investment because of the economic downturn as well as integrity lapses in the parties involved. I don't know how Marydel had such keen discernment, but her observations of the people we were dealing with were superior to mine. I know she has developed this skill over time, and I am glad I listened to her sound judgment!

People often equate skill in communication with being articulate and persuasive. More important than those attributes, however, is the quiet part of communication. It is the listening, watching, seeking first to understand before being understood, and discerning motivation. When we determine to develop these quiet skills, asking the Lord for his help, we gain far more than the flashy person with a glib tongue; we make a habit of discernment and sound judgment.

WORTH THE EFFORT

When we cultivate the good habits we talked about in this chapter, we are developing characteristics that make us excellent leaders and faithful stewards in God's kingdom. Some of these habits will be more difficult than others and must be developed over a long period of time through focus and repetitive action. I have found, however, that all of them are worthy of the effort.

Keep in mind that only negative habits come naturally and easily. As sinful creatures, our default tendencies include selfishness, laziness, pride, and foolishness. The good news is that the Holy Spirit gives us power to repent, turn away from these, and develop a righteous life that supports an effective business in God's economy.

CHAPTER 6

AVOID THESE THINGS

Destructive Behaviors

A casual reading of the book of Proverbs may not reveal the things that displease God. However, it becomes obvious upon closer reading that there are things God condemns or warns us about. It wasn't until meditating on some of those verses that I realized how sternly God warns us about certain sins and people.

American culture celebrates proud, self-made men and women. Obviously these attitudes are the opposite of the humble attitude God loves and calls us to embrace. Look carefully through the following list and note how many of these things are promoted in our entertainment and advertising:

- Wicked, evil, violent, and perverse people
- Foolish people
- The rejection of wisdom

- Pride and arrogance
- Anger
- Adultery and improper sexual activity
- Untruthfulness and lying
- Disputes, quarrels, gossip, lawsuits, and strife
- Excessive drinking
- The pursuit of getting rich (greed)

As we develop our faith, we realize the meaning behind fearing God. It is to our benefit to take each of these warnings seriously, as doing so will protect us from the unanticipated but devastating consequences of sinful people, attitudes, and behaviors.

AVOID WICKED, EVIL, VIOLENT, AND PERVERSE PEOPLE: DON'T EVEN GO NEAR 'EM

Proverbs repeatedly warns us against the wicked, their enticements, their deceptions, and their entanglements. The following verses make me shudder at the consequences of failing to heed God's loving warnings:

- The sinful ambush themselves and lose their lives to ill-gotten gain (1:10-19).
- Wicked people walk in dark and devious ways, rejoicing in the perverseness of evil (2:12-15).
- *"Do not envy the violent or choose any of their ways"* (3:31).

- Perverse people pursue twisted values (16:27-30). Their way *"is like deep darkness; they do not know what makes them stumble"* (4:19).
- Keep away from perversity and corrupt talk (4:24).
- The perverse man or woman stirs up conflict (16:28).
- The Lord hates *"haughty eyes, a lying tongue, hands that shed innocent blood, a heart that devises wicked schemes, feet that are quick to rush into evil, a false witness who pours out lies and a person who stirs up conflict in the community"* (6:16-19).
- Avoid cruel, wicked, evil people whose hearts are perverse (11:17-21).
- No one can be established through wickedness. He or she will be overthrown and eliminated (12:3,7).
- *"Evildoers are trapped by their sinful talk"* (12:13).
- The wicked bring shame and disgrace and are detestable in God's eyes (13:5; 15:9; 21:27).
- Avoid malicious people whose hearts harbor deceit and abominations; their deception and wickedness will be exposed (26:24-26).
- *"Evildoers do not understand what is right"* and *"are snared by their own sin"* (28:5; 29:6).
- *"When the wicked thrive, so does sin"* (29:16).
- *"The wicked detest the upright"* (29:27).

As you can see from this long list, the Lord is serious about avoiding these types of people. We are told to not even *"set foot on the path of the wicked or walk in the way of evildoers"* (4:14).

We should be proactive about avoiding evil people because of the devastation they cause. We are to look for a way to escape if we encounter them.

No one wants to become entangled with perverse people who plot harm, engage in violence, bend the truth, or falsely accuse, but there is a subtle danger of doing so. It's possible to be lured into doing business with someone like this without knowing the depth of their deviousness. Their rationalizations appeal to our own desire for gain, numbing us to the cry of our conscience.

Even though the rewards they offer may be enticing, these people don't deliver what they offer. It does not benefit us to even briefly associate with them. God says don't listen to them, don't envy them, don't imitate them, don't associate with them. Handle them like deadly poison in pretty bottles. Evil, wicked people do not have a future hope (24:20). Sure, they hope like everyone else, but God says their hope is misplaced and bankrupt; it will not mature into reality. In the end, their evil deeds will ensnare them and deliver them to destruction. The pit they dig is the very one they'll fall into (26:27).

My travels in third-world countries have shown me how evil leaders oppress their people in all the ways God warns us to avoid. Genocide, mutilation, torture, and abuses of every kind, unthinkable in our culture, are commonplace when wicked people are in power. They refuse to do what is right (21:7), and *"when the wicked rise to power, people go into hiding"* (28:12,28). When evil people rule a country, many flee to save their own lives.

Wicked rulers oppress helpless people (28:15), because they do not care for the poor (29:7). As a result, the economy suffers and sin thrives (29:16). Detesting the upright (29:27), wicked rulers fight against justice to keep their position, but there is no future hope for them (24:20). God may thwart their efforts on earth, but even if he doesn't, they will certainly be judged in the end.

In contrast, there is hope for those in God's economy— both present and future hope.

AVOID FOOLISH PEOPLE: SAND IN YOUR SHOES

Proverbs has this to say about fools and foolishness (or folly).

- Avoid foolish people (14:7; 26:6-12).
- *"Do not speak to fools"* (23:9).
- You will not remove the folly from a fool (27:22).
- *"Fools give full vent to their rage"* (29:11).
- *"Stone is heavy and sand a burden, but a fool's provocation is heavier than both"* (27:3).

"A fool's provocation" is worth addressing. I've been provoked by men who had foolish ideas and insisted on their execution. The burden I felt was exactly like a stone around my neck or walking through soft sand (27:3). As a former scout-master, I led many adventure outings with young men. I remember one particular backpacking trip through a historic gold miners' trail in Alaska. At the end of a long day, after a laborious climb over rocks and up steep inclines, we hiked a mile through soft sand. Already fatigued and weighed down by the heavy pack on my shoulders, it was very provoking to have to hike that last mile through sand. Every step took twice the effort of walking on normal ground. I feel the same kind of irritation and exhaustion when foolish people do not listen to counsel or simply reject it.

We are to stay away from fools because wisdom and knowledge aren't found in them and because their actions lead to folly that will ensnare us. When I was in college, I was influenced by many buddies who thought the greatest reward in life was to go out drinking. As you can imagine—or may have seen for yourself—foolish people can influence us to make all kinds of poor choices. They always seem to be in trouble and fail to learn from their mistakes. They typically have an arsenal of excuses, but we need to recognize their poor judgment and flawed decisions for what they are. Companionship with fools is foolishness by association.

It is just as foolish to think that if we travel extensively and are not accountable to the people who know us well, we will avoid the temptation of doing foolish things. I've traveled with several men who hit the bars or strip clubs late at night. This is a dangerous position to be in; my social sensitivities to them can lead to moral insensitivities. If I am unable to disassociate from these types of people, I must draw clear boundaries and pay the price for adhering to them. I must also fly the flag high and early, not in a self-righteous manner, but in a way that protects my spouse, my company, and my reputation.

Because we will definitely encounter foolish people in business, we must devise a strategy for dealing with them. We want to treat fools in a way that honors God while protecting us from being caught in their folly.

LISTENING TO FOLLY:
THE REJECTION OF WISDOM

A major theme throughout the book of Proverbs is the contrast between two voices. One is Wisdom, calling aloud for the righteous to follow (8:1-11). She raises her voice to all human-kind to speak what is right, true, and just. She speaks to all who are discerning and encourages those who listen to choose her instruction. She claims that nothing compares to her in value.

The other voice is Folly, calling out to fools who reject Wisdom. Those who reject Wisdom in favor of Folly choose a path that leads to early death (9:13-18). Calamity will overtake them and disaster will sweep them away. They will look for Wisdom but will not find her, because they have spurned her call, opting instead for the easy, crooked way. They will eat the fruit of their schemes, eventually leading to the complacency that will destroy them (1:20-33).

Both Wisdom and Folly vie for the attention of a person's heart. Those who choose Wisdom will reap eternal rewards because they have had the discernment to follow God's principles. Those who follow the voice of Folly chase after the deception of worldly pleasures that lead to the grave. Throughout

Proverbs, an adulterer is the lure that draws the foolish person away from God's principles to follow the sensual desires of the heart.

In the business world, both voices call loudly. In the world's economy, Folly offers instant gratification and pleasure, usually through a perversion of some good thing God created. Anything divorced from its intended design or from God's character, however, will eventually lead to destruction and even death.

In contrast, Wisdom's benefits have a more obvious price tag, one that is clearly shown up front. Typically, the price has to be paid in advance, trusting that the Designer's plan is worth the cost. No deception here: There is a clear price, and, if anything, the benefits to follow are *understated*. If we believe what Solomon wrote, wisdom is the greatest thing we can desire.

When businesspeople fail to seek godly counsel or collective wisdom, they are rejecting an instrument God has provided to keep them from folly.

AVOID PRIDE AND ARROGANCE:
PRIDE ALWAYS GOES BEFORE A FALL

God hates pride. At the root of virtually every other sin, pride exalts itself above God, contaminating his good creation with perversion and decay. Arrogant people consistently resist God's authority and superiority with their assertion that they know better. This never produces good results, for them or anyone else. No wonder *"the LORD detests all the proud of heart"* (Proverbs 16:5).

As evidenced in the *Wall Street Journal*, business magazines, and news broadcasts, people who have amassed a fortune are touted and honored in our society. Just like overglorified professional athletes, founders of successful companies are viewed as heroes on the basis of accomplishments that are shallow and short-lived even from a human perspective, let alone an eternal one.

Many believe their own press releases and consequently are full of pride and self-promotion. They fail to recognize that God is the one who has given them their abilities and allowed them to succeed, and their egotism is a personal affront to him. Proverbs says, *"The LORD tears down the house of the proud"* (15:25). In other words, God will tear down the business built on an individual's ego and pride. God not only laments the arrogant attitude but also hates the pride that comes from deep within the heart; it does not go unpunished. *"Pride goes before destruction, a haughty spirit before a fall"* (16:18).

Businessmen and women need to take seriously the following warnings about pride:

- God mocks the proud but gives favor to the humble (3:34).
- God hates pride and arrogance (8:13).
- Pride breeds strife (13:10).
- *"The LORD detests all the proud of heart. Be sure of this: They will not go unpunished"* (16:5).
- *"Before a downfall the heart is haughty, but humility comes before honor"* (18:12).

- *"Haughty eyes and a proud heart . . . produce sin"* (21:4).
- *"The proud and arrogant person . . . behaves with insolent fury"* (21:24).
- Don't exalt yourself or claim a place among great men and women (25:6-7).
- *"It's not good to seek honors for yourself"* (25:27, NLT).
- *"Do you see a person wise in their own eyes? There is more hope for a fool than for them"* (26:12).
- *"Pride brings a person low, but the lowly in spirit gain honor"* (29:23).

Pride is not always overt. It can be subtle. Subtle pride sometimes shows itself as a refusal to respond to counsel or to a rebuke from a caring friend. This stubbornness leads to self-reliance of a dangerous kind. *"Those who trust in themselves are fools"* (28:26). I have seen people agree verbally and then leave the room and act in contradiction to their agreement. Their refusal to follow the advice of their counselors reveals a dangerous delusion: "I'm right and everyone else is wrong." Prevalent among some strong-willed leaders, business founders, and entrepreneurs, this stubborn pride is a perversion of healthy conviction and passion.

Pride can also be the cause of conflicts with others. This has been true for me. When I feel rubbed the wrong way by others, I usually notice that they happen to be much like me. The things I don't like about them are the things I battle within myself. Arrogantly judging others this way creates wedges in relationships and leads to conflict.

To counteract pride, we must learn the meaning and application of humility and service to others. God gives grace to the humble, and many times we need this grace to help us overcome our own egotism and stubbornness. I seem to have fewer conflicts when I am humble and submit myself to others, showing them respect and unconditional love.

I have often wondered why God hates pride and arrogance so much. I believe it's because thinking more highly of ourselves than we ought is a form of rebellion deep within our hearts, an attempt to be in control of our lives without being submissive or obedient to the one who made us. As a business founder and entrepreneur, I've struggled with pride and arrogance, thinking I was accomplishing something great. I learned early that this attitude is displeasing to God.

While still in college, I asked God for two things: "Please don't make me rich, and please don't make me famous." That was my way of asking him to keep me from pride and self-promotion. In my profession, it is easy to seek recognition for your design talent in outstanding projects as confirmation of success. I've always desired to be recognized by my professional society as being outstanding, but I don't want public recognition to influence me to become proud. Prominence in itself may not be a problem, but when your opinion of yourself is based on your accomplishments and fanfare, your values and priorities need revision.

True humility is a valuable asset, but false humility is a subtle form of pride. My wife helped me recognize the false humility in my decision to buy an inexpensive subcompact car under the guise of being a good steward. In reality, it was more about false humility than frugality.

Marydel never did like my subcompact car, especially because I did not get her counsel prior to buying it. I simply drove it home, grinning ear to ear, expecting her approval because I was "so humble in buying an economy car." But my false humility began to surface when I told people about how I drove this economy car to save money. I wanted others to notice that although I had the means to drive a much nicer car, I had chosen to be a "humble" man.

Marydel, in her typical wise discernment, didn't criticize me. She let it work itself out, and eventually I realized my false humility for what it was. I asked for forgiveness, and then I asked her to help me select a more appropriate car. She did, and I've never enjoyed a car so much.

AVOID ANGER: CHECK IT AT THE DOOR

How many times have we dealt with angry people in business? Whether blatant or subtle, their anger stirs up conflict all around them. I have dealt with many clients who responded with anger when things were not going well or according to their preconceived plan. This is uncomfortable for both parties, often damaging the working relationship. Proverbs advises us to carefully control our anger and avoid those who cannot.

Anger can be contagious, and no business wants a culture that is characterized by it. Proverbs gives a lot of instruction for avoiding this slippery slope. *"A gentle answer turns away wrath, but a harsh word stirs up anger"* (15:1). *"A hot-tempered person stirs up conflict, but the one who is patient calms a quarrel"* (15:18). *"A quick-tempered person does foolish things"* (14:17).

Avoiding a culture of anger requires consistently controlling our emotional reactions so we don't incite others to frustration, quarrels, and dissension. Business pressures often fray our nerves and make us edgy. As soon as we notice the first hint of anger, we need to step back and ask God to give us his perspective and peace. If we don't do this early in the process, we can easily get to the point where we don't want peace; we just want to vent. I can't recall the last time I saw raw venting contribute anything good to a tense situation.

- *"Starting a quarrel is like breaching a dam; so drop the matter before a dispute breaks out"* (17:14).
- *"Even fools are thought wise if they keep silent, and discerning if they hold their tongues"* (17:28).
- *"Anger is cruel"* (27:4).
- *"An angry person stirs up conflict"* (29:22).

Proverbs tells us to not make friends with people who are hot-tempered (22:24). We are not even to associate with those who are easily angered, not only because they stir up dissension and commit many sins but also because their uncontrolled emotion can be contagious. *"Fools give full vent to their rage, but the wise bring calm in the end"* (29:11).

Years ago I had an office worker who was adept at avoiding anger and promoting peace in all situations. Her calm, positive manner when demanding clients called was like oil in a neglected engine, soothing the friction and reducing the heat. I learned from her example and have applied it in the many years since her departure from the firm.

I've taken many calls from frustrated and, at times, angry clients. The calls rarely had anything to do with the personal aspect of our relationship; they were generally in response to problems on a project—problems that raised fears of costly delays or worse. I've learned that my response makes all the difference. If I match their emotion and respond in a defensive manner, it escalates the tension and makes the underlying problem difficult to address logically. If I remain calm and humbly listen, however, they frequently settle down quickly, enabling us to resolve the issue together.

When dealing with people who are angry about some-thing, I first work hard at understanding their perspective. Once I understand that, it is much easier to understand their emotions. When I can communicate back to them their perspective and its understandable emotion, they relax in the confidence that I care and will do my best to resolve their concern. When they feel understood, most people are willing to consider another perspective or a variety of constructive solu-tions. A careful, gentle response truly turns away the anger and wrath of the other party (Proverbs 15:1).

So check your anger at the door. It's important to do so every time you open the door to your workplace. Customers are never impressed with your anger, but they will always be impressed with kindness and self-control.

AVOID IMPROPER SENSUAL ACTIVITY: FIRE IN YOUR LAP

Along with power and money, sex is an area at the top of the list when it comes to classic areas of moral business failure. Proverbs deals with all three, warning us that our egos tend to misuse power, our greed leads us to misuse money, and our lust draws us to inappropriate sexual relationships. Large portions of Proverbs 5–7 warn of the destructive forces of adultery and improper sexual relationships.

Our society has lost the restraining influence of cultural taboos against sensual indiscretions; what was once considered unacceptable behavior now seems commonplace and easily discounted. Extramarital relationships in the workplace, whether sexual or emotional, are as great a temptation for Christians as for those without faith. Aggravated by explicit advertisements in all forms of media, sexual promiscuity seems to be acceptable and even promoted.

Improper sexual activity blinds clear thinking, business judgment, and the consideration of its consequences. The worst business decision a man or woman can make is to have a sexual—or emotionally intimate—relationship with a person other than his or her spouse. No one who goes there escapes unpunished (Proverbs 7:10-27). Businesspeople young and old should take heed, because many fall to these temptations in later life. Temptations do not become easier with time, as is evidenced by so many broken homes.

Improper sexual activity begins with lust that captivates the unguarded heart and leads to fire. Proverbs asks, *"Can a man scoop fire into his lap without his clothes being burned? Can a man walk on hot coals without his feet being scorched?"* (6:27-28). That's a graphic description of what happens sooner or later in any illicit relationship.

Lust in the heart can be fueled by pornography. Our company fights hard to prevent pornography from entering our business culture. Office computers can easily become infested in spite of most companies having policies against viewing pornography at work. The temptation is always real and available when "no one is looking." For that reason I've come to the decision that when I travel on business, I don't even turn on the TV. By refusing to watch TV, I'm protecting my heart from impurities that can lead to lust. I'm not suggesting that everything on TV is bad, but a lack of accountability is a slippery slope. Better to set a boundary well back from the point of danger.

In proper context sex is a holy activity ordained and blessed by God. Outside of his design, however, it becomes illicit and dangerous. These same problems were common in Solomon's day, leading him to devote considerable space to warning us about the dangers of having an affair:

- The adulteress ignores her covenant with her husband (Proverbs 2:16-17).
- Keep away from the wayward woman. *"Do not lust in your heart after her beauty"* (6:25).
- Adultery ends in utter ruin (5:1-11). Adultery will cost a man all his wealth; he has no sense and destroys

himself (6:31-32). *"His shame will never be wiped away"* (6:33).

- Keep away from the adulteress (7:5; 30:20) and her seductive words, as adultery is a highway to the grave and a chamber of death (7:22-27). Avoid the wayward wife (23:27-28).
- *"The mouth of the adulteress is a deep pit; a man who is under the LORD's wrath falls into it"* (22:14).

While traveling several years ago, I noticed a helpless bird frantically flying around inside the high ceilings of the airport. It seemed terrified, never stopping but hopelessly darting from one portion of the ceiling structure to another. Men and women who stray from home are like a bird straying from its nest (27:8). They are vulnerable to dangerous sexual temptation. We must guard home with all vigilance, letting neither our heart nor our actions lead us astray from devoting ourselves to our spouse and children.

AVOID LYING: "THE TRUTH, THE WHOLE TRUTH, SO HELP ME, GOD!"

Many years ago a boss gave me a great piece of advice that parallels many proverbs: "Lying is easier at first but harder in the end, because you have to remember each one! Eventually, you'll forget one and the whole thing will unravel." When it's tempting to get out of a problem by not revealing the whole truth, we should stop and realize that lies—and half-truths—always catch up with us. And as we have all seen, the cover-up is often more damaging than the mistake, because it is clearly deliberate.

Proverbs makes it clear that the Lord finds lying detestable (12:22). We must take heed when God speaks so strongly against these things:

- *"The LORD hates . . . a lying tongue"* (6:16-17).
- *"The LORD hates . . . a false witness who pours out lies"* (6:16,19).
- *"A false witness will not go unpunished, and whoever pours out lies will perish"* (19:9).
- *"Differing weights and differing measures—the LORD detests them both"* (20:10; see also 20:23). This is basic dishonesty and lack of integrity.
- *"A fortune made by a lying tongue is a fleeting vapor and a deadly snare"* (21:6).
- *"A false witness will perish"* (21:28).
- False testimony against your neighbor is a deceitful and deadly weapon (25:18).
- *"A lying tongue hates those it hurts, and a flattering mouth works ruin"* (26:28).

Lying, untruthfulness, stretching the truth, and gray areas are a tremendous problem in operating a business. During the mediation hearing mentioned earlier, my partner, Shade, and I expected the whole truth of the incident to be revealed. Not being experienced in mediation hearings, we were surprised to realize that truthfulness and full disclosure are not the norm for all parties. We saw the high-stakes game being played by legal guns hired to protect whoever paid them, presenting only the facts that would favor them while deliberately omitting the facts that would expose their fabricated case.

We understood the situation, and we were confident that if the facts were properly presented, the liability would fall on the appropriate shoulders. We also knew there was professional pride involved, and we did not want to embarrass or discredit our client. Throughout this hearing we had the sense that our client's attorney recognized our desire for truthfulness and appreciated our integrity to present the facts as we knew them. We endeavored to do this without regard to our own personal liability. Our position was that if we were at fault, we would take responsibility. If we weren't, the responsibility should rest on others.

In the world's economy, many transactions occur without full disclosure or truthfulness. We see this when a car dealer fails to mention that the car has been wrecked and repaired or when a real estate agent does not reveal that the house has a history of flooding issues, or when an architect tells clients and customers what they want to hear rather than the bad news. When we present half-truths or withhold information, we are not telling the truth. Anything less than the full truth is not really the truth. Deliberate omissions are the same as telling a lie. God hates this and wants us to have no part in it.

If we would stop and realize how much God hates untruthfulness, we would run from it, in business and elsewhere.

We rarely think about the ramifications of lying, because in the world's economy, it only seems to matter if you get caught, and no one ever intends to get caught. But even if we don't get caught, the ramifications are devastating. Lying displeases God, rots our character, destroys our integrity, and cripples our testimony.

We cannot live a righteous life when we occasionally or conveniently lie; we must always tell the truth, regardless of the consequences. Considering that the day is coming when everything secret will be publicly exposed in the full light of God's knowledge, would you rather be one who dies for telling the truth or one who gets away with a lie—for a while? When there is no hiding place and the truth is exposed, the consequences will not be temporary; they will have eternal impact.

AVOID DISPUTES, QUARRELS, GOSSIP, LAWSUITS, AND STRIFE: BREACHING A DAM

"Starting a quarrel is like breaching a dam" (Proverbs 17:14). We can all remember the devastation caused by the breach in the New Orleans levees after Hurricane Katrina. Once the levees gave way, the water couldn't be stopped until it settled in every low point without regard to what it displaced. Years later, some neighborhoods are still dominated by abandoned houses and empty lots.

Imagine that kind of damage the next time you are tempted to start or prolong a quarrel. Giving in to the momentary rush of emotion—like a storm swell—doesn't solve anything; it only puts everything downstream at risk. Proverbs wisely advises us to *"drop the matter before a dispute breaks out"* (17:14).

Quarrels and disputes, along with gossip, damage relationships with coworkers, employees, and clients as well as those on the periphery who observe. We may never be aware of all the damage caused, but God sees it all and grieves over the unnecessary pain; he hates disrupted unity.

- *"The LORD hates . . . a person who stirs up conflict in the community"* (Proverbs 6:16,19).
- A perverse or hot-tempered person stirs up conflict (15:18; 16:28).
- *"Evildoers foster rebellion"* (or dissension) (17:11).
- *"A hot-tempered person must pay the penalty"* (19:19).
- *"It is to one's honor to avoid strife, but every fool is quick to quarrel"* (20:3).
- A quarrelsome person kindles strife (26:21).
- Avoid gossip (26:20,22).
- Rebellion leads to disorder and many rulers (28:2).
- *"The greedy stir up conflict"* (28:25).
- Avoid stirring up anger, which produces strife (30:33).

Gossip can easily become part of the corporate culture. We have all experienced the pain of gossip, and most of us have been guilty of initiating it at one time or another. No matter how subtle or carefully rationalized, gossip and its cousin innuendo destroy unity. Gossip undermines a business culture by destroying teamwork and the desire to serve one another within the business. My business partners and I work hard to squelch gossip, making it clear to our employees that we will not tolerate this toxin. As the proverb says, *"The words of a gossip are like choice morsels; they go down to the inmost parts"* (26:22).

Unity is more important than talent in the success of a firm. Fighting within our ranks makes it difficult to perform professionally. We've seen the misery it has caused everyone—including our clients—when we've had employees who created dissension for their own benefit. One of the hardest things a leader does is confront problems of strife and lack of unity within his or her personnel, but it is one of our most important tasks.

"A brother wronged is more unyielding than a fortified city; disputes are like the barred gates of a citadel" (18:19). When we quarrel, everyone puts up their defenses. We may become unapproachable or unyielding, refusing to listen to the other side.

When business disagreements escalate, pride is certain to be an influence—if not the whole cause. With neither party backing down and emotions ratcheting up, disputes lead to lawsuits, offended parties, and broken relationships. Sometimes discernment leads us to back down when we shouldn't have to. We could have won our mediation case, for instance, and not have had to pay anything, but the long-term result wouldn't have been as good.

I have found it is always best to be at peace with everyone, seeking to resolve issues before quarrels develop. This is not easy, especially when you're sure you're right. But it's always better to approach problems logically as coseekers of a solution rather than emotionally as adversaries. *"It is to one's honor to avoid strife"* (20:3).

AVOID EXCESSIVE DRINKING: ONE TOO MANY

Many business cultures are built upon the bond of drinking together. While the Bible does not condemn drinking alcohol, it does condemn drunkenness. Because of the inherent dangers of alcoholism, many Christ followers have strong convictions against drinking at all, but the Bible doesn't go that far. Proverbs clearly cautions against drinking that impairs judgment or becomes a focus.

- Whoever is led astray by beer and wine is not wise (20:1).
- *"Whoever loves wine and olive oil will never be rich"* (21:17).
- *"Do not join those who drink too much wine or gorge themselves on meat"* (23:20).
- *"Drunkards and gluttons become poor, and drowsiness clothes them in rags"* (23:21).
- Don't linger over wine; *"in the end it bites like a snake and poisons like a viper"* (23:32).
- It's not for kings to drink wine or for rulers to crave beer (31:4-5).

RICH AND FAMOUS:
THE PURSUIT OF GETTING RICH

Nearly anyone who has seriously read the Bible knows the warnings against striving to get rich. Many pitfalls await the young businessperson in this pursuit. When getting rich is the goal, it is easy to forget that God is the giver of wealth. This simple shift of focus may seem insignificant, but it destroys a person's priorities. That, from God's perspective, is the deal breaker.

Put yourself in God's position for a moment. I know our poor imaginations can't match his reality, but I think this exercise has value. Suppose you were extremely wealthy and you fell in love. In contemplation of marriage, suppose you offered your potential spouse the choice of taking you without your wealth or taking your wealth instead of you. If that seems farfetched, why do you think the marriages of so many wealthy people are preceded by prenuptial agreements?

God, who loves us purely, knows our best interests are served only in relationship with him. When anything else, including the pursuit of wealth, takes priority over our devotion to him, we settle for a perversion of the perfect good he intends for us. Just as lust is a perversion of love, wealth prioritized ahead of God becomes toxic and delivers pain rather than joy.

Greed is a fuel that ignites the passion to become rich. This passion often causes people to damage their family relationships through neglect. Ironically, it can also lead to financial disaster for a family: *"The greedy bring ruin to their households"*

(Proverbs 15:27). God's warning to avoid greed—like every warning he issues—is for our protection.

Some people say they don't want to become rich, they just want enough money to "be comfortable." By "comfortable," however, they usually mean wealthy enough to never worry about money. But most of the world's wealthiest obsess over money; they just do it in a different way and for a different reason. If they haven't learned contentment—the ability to not worry about money regardless of what they have—no amount of money will give it to them.

Unless we view money as God intended within his economy, we'll likely worry about it, violating his warnings in Proverbs:

- Whoever trusts in riches will fall (11:28).
- *"The greedy bring ruin to their households"* (15:27).
- *"Do not wear yourself out to get rich. . . . Cast but a glance at riches, and they are gone, for they will surely sprout wings and fly off to the sky like an eagle"* (23:4-5).
- *"Riches do not endure forever"* (27:24).
- *"A faithful person will be richly blessed, but one eager to get rich will not go unpunished"* (28:20).
- *"The stingy are eager to get rich and are unaware that poverty awaits them"* (28:22).
- *"The greedy stir up conflict"* (28:25).

The pursuit of getting rich can lead to oppressing others. *"Whoever increases wealth by taking interest or profit from the*

poor amasses it for another, who will be kind to the poor" (28:8).
We are warned to never exploit the needy, thereby taking
advantage of them. The Lord will take up their case and will
plunder the oppressor. The disadvantaged are vulnerable to
abuse. In God's economy, the businessperson is to protect them,
remembering that God is their defender.

The pursuit of wealth for the purpose of becoming
self-sufficient is outside the purpose for wealth in God's economy. Wealth was created by God, and he gives it to wise people
at his pleasure. Although being wealthy is not wrong, its use
outside of God's design is wrong. If we believe God owns the
world and everything in it, we must also believe he grants the
use of his wealth and in return expects businesspeople to be
stewards. I think the pursuit of getting rich often has more to
do with desire for selfish gain than desire to distribute it as a
good and faithful steward. We are told in Proverbs that God
gives wealth to the wise man. This wealth appears in many
forms: money, assets, and valuable objects, to name a few. But
it also includes time, talents, a person's essence, and all the
other attributes God uses to complete the good steward. God
bestows whatever wealth he chooses on faithful stewards;
he advises us to seek the wealth of wisdom and leave the rest
to him.

In Proverbs 30:7-9, the author asks two things from the
Lord: to keep falsehood from him, and to give him neither
poverty nor riches. Think about it; these are requested to
prevent dishonoring God. When that is our priority, we are free
to experience whatever blessing God chooses to release through

us. He knows we won't hoard it to our own detriment and the neglect of those he puts in our path.

TAKE HEED

Everything God warns us against takes us—and our businesses—in the direction of destruction. We know God reigns over heaven and earth, and in the end he will make all things new. But until then, we need to take each of these warnings seriously and avoid these kinds of people and sins at all costs.

CHAPTER 7

BECOME THESE THINGS

Characteristics

Have you considered the deep, soul-searching question, would I want to deal with myself in business? This question strikes at the heart of the young businessman and woman.

While Proverbs discusses many great characteristics of the heart, five stand out as particularly valuable to the person who wants to live a righteous life and operate successfully in God's economy. We are to become:

- Wise
- Humble
- Honest
- Prudent
- Diligent

As we apply the truth God has given us, we develop

wisdom that makes us more open to receiving instruction, rebuke, and correction. We never outgrow the need for God's correction; wisdom goes hand in hand with accepting and applying it. Without **humility**, our ego gets in the way and hardens us in our blind spots. Without **honesty** and integrity, we cannot operate for long in God's economy. If we are to be successful with the resources entrusted to us, we need **prudence** to maintain and multiply these resources. Prudence is the discretion and careful forethought that grows with experience and prepares us for future events. Finally, Proverbs says we are to show **diligence** in our work.

I have previously touched on some of these characteristics; however, because of their importance in developing the heart of the young businessperson, I want to review them.

BECOME WISE:
LOOK AT BUSINESS FROM GOD'S PERSPECTIVE

Again, God is the one who grants us wisdom, and when he gives businessmen and women insight into his kingdom, they begin living in eternity while on earth. Rather than thinking merely in terms of this short life, they measure everything with an eternal tape measure that uses infinity as a benchmark.

Wise businessmen and women look at their business from God's perspective. They learn to see things from his viewpoint and operate by his principles.

We can recognize a wise person by the following characteristics:

- *"The wise listen and add to their learning"*; they remain teachable (Proverbs 1:5). They heed instruction (13:1) and *"store up knowledge"* (10:14). *"By paying attention to the wise [the simple] get knowledge"* (21:11).

- The wise listen to counsel (2:1-5; 24:6) and take advice (13:10). They listen to rebukes from others, becoming wiser still (9:8-10; 10:8; 15:31).

- The wise have discretion to protect them and understanding to guard them from wicked people and the adulterer (2:11-17). *"The wise in heart are called discerning"* (16:21).

- Wisdom's teaching and commands bring peace and prosperity (3:2). The wise are blessed and receive favor from the Lord (3:13; 8:35). In the house of the wise are wonderful possessions (21:20).

- *"The wise inherit honor"* (3:35).

- The wise have knowledge, discretion, counsel, sound judgment, insight, and power (8:12-14).

- The wise *"walk in the way of righteousness, along the paths of justice"* (8:20). The wise are peacemakers, appeasing wrath (16:13-14). The wise walk with other wise people (13:20). The wise are patient and *"overlook an offense"* (19:11).

- The wise *"hold their tongues"* (10:19), and their hearts guide their mouths (16:23). *"The wise turn away anger"* (29:8). *"The wise bring calm in the end"* (29:11).

- *"The wise fear the LORD"* (14:16).

- The wise do not put up security for debts (22:26).
- The wise do not drink too much (23:20).

Notice that *"riches and honor, enduring wealth and prosperity"* accompany wisdom (8:18). Wisdom bestows *"a rich inheritance on those who love [her] and [makes] their treasuries full"* (8:21). The one with true wisdom understands that God designed wealth to be managed for his glory. Therefore, wise business-people are the best candidates to become stewards of wealth.

BECOME HUMBLE: DON'T TOOT YOUR OWN HORN

When I was a boy, my mom often said, "Don't toot your own horn." To me, this meant don't promote yourself or brag about your accomplishments; don't exalt yourself in front of others, and don't claim to be great. This was her way of teaching me the concept of becoming humble. In other words, let another praise you, don't praise yourself.

Proverbs has similar expressions:

- It is better for others to put you in a place of honor than for you to be asked to step aside and be humiliated before them (25:6-7).
- *"It's not good to seek honors for yourself"* (25:27, NLT).
- *"Do not boast about tomorrow, for you do not know what a day may bring"* (27:1).
- *"Let someone else praise you, and not your own mouth"* (27:2).

In addition, Proverbs has this to say about humility:

- *"Better to be a nobody [humble person] and yet have a servant than pretend to be somebody and have no food"* (12:9). *"One person pretends to be rich, yet has nothing; another [humble person] pretends to be poor, yet has great wealth"* (13:7).
- *"Humility comes before honor"* (15:33; 18:12).
- *"Humility is the fear of the LORD; its wages are riches and honor and life"* (22:4).
- Do not be wise in your own eyes (26:12).
- *"The lowly in spirit [humble] gain honor"* (29:23).
- *"With humility comes wisdom"* (11:2).

There is more to humility than not bragging about yourself. I have heard it said that humility is "knowing who God is and knowing who I am." Humility is knowing our awesome God on a personal, intimate level while maintaining full awareness of our complete dependence on him as recipients of his unmerited favor.

The enemy of humility is pride. Pride is putting ourselves ahead of others and rebelling against God. We have seen how much God despises these attitudes. Because he created us, it is inappropriate for us to be prideful or arrogant in front of him. How have you felt when you've had to deal with arrogant people? Didn't you find them offensive? I'm sure God views us in the same manner when we are rebellious rather than submissive to him.

Humility has been an important virtue in our company, best exemplified by the concept of "flying below the radar." Flying below the radar means avoiding attention that might endanger the mission. This keeps our egos in check. We want to discern the difference between professional pride, which is desirable, and personal pride (egotism), which is distasteful. We want to be known for humbly serving our clients, our vendors, and our outside consultants.

While it is desirable to be recognized as outstanding professionals, sometimes recognition carries the risk of egotism. By staying humble and resisting the urge to feed our egos, we can avoid some of the pitfalls of pride and arrogance.

BE HONEST: ARE YOU A PERSON OF INTEGRITY IN ALL CIRCUMSTANCES?

When I ask myself whether I would want to deal with myself in business, it is a real gut check.

Most of the time it's easy for me to be honest, but there are also times when I have not been accountable and I was tempted to be dishonest. I began to realize that God always wants our honesty, and we are always accountable to him. Although our actions are not always in full view of others, they are always within his view. Honesty in all circumstances is hard, but worth the effort.

God wants us to embrace the things he loves, including the honesty that reflects his character.

- *"Truthful lips endure forever"* (Proverbs 12:19).
- *"The LORD detests lying lips, but he delights in people who are trustworthy"* (12:22). Numerous proverbs tell us how much the Lord hates dishonesty, particularly lying, in business.
- There is great value in *"the one who speaks what is right"* (16:13).
- *"Honest scales and balances belong to the LORD"* (16:11).
- *"The LORD detests dishonest scales, but accurate weights find favor with him"* (11:1; see also 20:10,23).

It's a common practice in business to treat people differently, using different standards. Proverbs deals with this issue by saying the Lord detests differing weights. In business, treating one vendor or supplier differently from another can lead to favoritism and potential dishonesty. God calls us to utmost honesty in dealing with all people. When setting the price for something in business, we should be fair to all. Honest pricing is a mandate exemplified by honest scales. In ancient times, dishonest businesspeople cheated customers by using false weights in their pursuit of extra profit. God detests cheating, and he fights to protect the innocent. I have no desire to provoke God to fight against me and the company he has helped me build. So I am careful to avoid under-the-table transactions as well as taking advantage of an uninformed or weaker person.

It can be tempting for professional service businesses to fudge on time sheets used to bill clients. "Rounding up" time may be common in the industry but is not permitted in our firm. My best employees are those who are meticulously honest with their time recording, particularly when it has financial implications. View it from the client's perspective: Wouldn't you want to be charged accurately? God calls us to be honest even when no one else will ever find out.

I have watched businesspeople present body language or facial expressions to change the meaning behind their verbal statements. The simple trick of rolling the eyes can communicate a lack of trust or support of an individual in spite of verbal affirmation. God, who examines the heart and knows the motives behind all our actions, calls us to total honesty.

Relational honesty carries its own set of difficulties. In many business cultures, politeness trumps honesty. Many times we do not express our actual intentions, either because it is to our advantage to be politically correct or because we are afraid of disagreeing with another person's opinion. I catch myself at times giving a politically correct answer in lieu of the truth.

Honesty cannot be separated from integrity. Anything that isn't the truth is detested by God, who is both grace and truth.

BE PRUDENT:
DON'T LEAVE MONEY AT THE OFFICE

Proverbs 8:12 says that wherever wisdom goes, prudence will closely follow.

- *"The prudent overlook an insult,"* not showing their annoyance quickly (12:16).

- *"The prudent keep their knowledge to themselves, but a fool's heart blurts out folly"* (12:23). Again we see the principles of self-control and listening more than talking.
- *"All who are prudent act with knowledge, but fools expose their folly"* (13:16). Prudence acts with wisdom rather than just emotion.
- *"The wisdom of the prudent is to give thought to their ways"* (14:8).
- *"The prudent give thought to their steps"* (14:15). Unlike the simple who believe anything, the prudent carefully consider, test, and evaluate before acting.
- *"The prudent are crowned with knowledge"* (14:18).
- The prudent heed correction. In other words, they don't spurn discipline but take correction seriously and implement it (15:5).
- *"The prudent see danger and take refuge"* (22:3). They look for signs to interpret and then make plans to avoid future problems.

As a young practitioner I was advised to "not leave money at the office." This wasn't a warning about thieves, but a caution against spending so much in overhead that it kills profit. By keeping our overhead low, we leave more money available for paychecks. This is prudence.

Consequently, I developed a conservative approach to office stewardship. Not only did we save rubber bands, we also saved paper clips and recycled the back of fax confirmation sheets for invoice copies. To this day we purchase limited office supplies, reuse everything we can, and recycle our waste products. By cutting expenses, recycling, reusing, and not remodeling our lease space every three years, we are able to provide bonuses for our employees. When business slows down, we cut our overhead to match our income. This practice keeps us profitable and avoids "leaving money at the office."

I have learned the value of not presuming on the future. Knowing that recessions are sure to come periodically, we make plans that enable us to take them in stride. A lease I signed twenty years ago provides a good example. This lease had the typical provision of increasing the rent every year, but I was uncomfortable with that feature because of the uncertainty of the future.

I inverted the lease rate so it would decline each year. Knowing that we currently had the money to cover the higher rate, I chose to pay it now rather than later when the economy might make it more difficult for us. I have continued this practice and benefited from a strengthened cash flow and sense of security, knowing my overhead will decrease over time. As a side note, I have remained in the same building for almost twenty-five years and pay the same comparable lease rate.

As a close companion to wisdom, prudence is a characteristic that should mark young businessmen and women. By it they will navigate the stormy waters of uncertainty so prevalent in the world's economy. Prudent businesspeople seek wisdom, applying the experiences and lessons learned in preparation for the future.

BE DILIGENT: COME IN EARLY TO MAKE UP FOR STAYING LATE

When I was a young intern architect in college, I worked for an established architect in Myrtle Beach, South Carolina. I had a lot to learn about becoming diligent. I remember arriving late one morning and working hard all day. As I was about to leave a little bit early, an older gentlemen said very softly, "Are you leaving early to make up for coming in late?"

Startled, I stopped dead in my tracks. He turned his head to continue working at his drafting table. I will never forget that rebuke. I have quoted it many times, encouraging young architects in our firm to learn the value of diligence.

Here is what Proverbs says about the diligent person:

- Those who work their land will have an abundance (12:11; 28:19).
- The work of a person's hand will reward him (12:14).
- *"Diligent hands will rule, but laziness ends in forced labor"* (12:24).
- *"The precious possession of a man is diligence"* (12:27, NASB).
- *"The desires of the diligent are fully satisfied"* (13:4).
- *"All hard work brings a profit"* (14:23).
- *"The plans of the diligent lead to profit as surely as haste leads to poverty"* (21:5).

Our firm's most diligent architects are also the most skilled architects. Skilled people, whose abilities are developed through hard work, will serve before "kings." Diligence and skill go hand in hand.

It has been our policy for many years to take the first flight out when traveling on company business. There are several reasons for this policy. It affords the staff the opportunity to get an early start. Airlines usually have an airplane ready to go for the first flight out each morning. If there are weather delays or problems, the traveler can usually catch another flight and still reach his destination in plenty of time to work. In addition, rising early in order to make the day more efficient and profitable fosters diligence. The basis for this policy permeates every part of the company. We are a firm known for efficiency and hard work. Our efficiencies have allowed us to master an architectural protocol that produces more projects with fewer people in less time. This enables us to meet demanding deadlines. Our firm's efficient work enables us to charge the client a smaller fee. Meanwhile, our professionalism drives us to provide quality service. This successful formula has allowed us to capture and maintain significant corporate clients.

SUCCESSFUL IN THE EYES OF THE CREATOR OF BUSINESS

While there are other great heart characteristics in the Proverbs that would be helpful to cultivate, a disciplined focus on becoming a person who is wise, humble, honest, prudent, and diligent will make you successful in the eyes of the Creator of business.

CHAPTER 8

A JOURNEY TOWARD STEWARDSHIP

My partner Shade O'Quinn and I boarded the plane to return home after our mediation hearing. We reflected on the day's activities and all that had happened in the three years since the roof collapse. We had endured many emotional peaks and valleys along the way, and now the stress of this incident was finally over. As we slumped comfortably in our seats, we felt the joy of knowing our mediation was settled in an amicable fashion. We were at peace with our client, our insurance company, and ourselves. Satisfied that we had achieved a win-win solution, we were overcome with gratitude.

The flight back home was a perfect opportunity to rewind the film from the vantage point of hindsight. Until this situation, we hadn't known such vulnerability, and we learned to trust God at a much deeper level during this desperate time.

Even so, we were unaware of how many of the Proverbs had been at work in our saga. It wasn't until later, after my three-year study of Proverbs, that I recognized how many of God's business principles were at work in that situation.

His protection had been evident. We felt his supernatural protection, particularly from the potential catastrophic loss we faced, a loss that could have amounted to millions of dollars.

He granted us wisdom in our recognition of the real purpose of the lawsuit. We realized the client was not angry with us. There was no vindictiveness or intent to hurt us; they simply wanted to recover their insurance deductible. The insurance company was covering the damaged merchandise along with the potential lost sales.

We applied the principle of generosity when we offered to settle despite having no liability for the roof collapse.

Discernment and sound judgment enabled us to evaluate the real issues and to understand the personalities involved in the mediation hearing. By understanding the issues important to each party, we were able to facilitate a quick resolution to the satisfaction of our client and their insurance company.

With hard work, we prepared for the case by doing extensive research and evaluations of the surrounding circumstances. **By being diligent** in our preparation, we were better able to see the facts of the case, respond during the mediation hearing, and defend ourselves along with our attorney.

We were prudent to ensure that we were handling ourselves in an appropriate manner, thus protecting our client relationship.

We avoided anger because we had developed self-control and were able to maintain a peaceful demeanor.

We demonstrated humility by keeping quiet when accused and listening respectfully to all parties during the deliberations.

The integrity of our actions resulted in the client realizing our intent to be honest and our willingness to take responsibility if necessary. Our client's attorney verbalized this at the end of our meeting and even called our client to express appreciation for our integrity.

We realized the value of counsel. We received advice not only from attorneys but from other consultants, our own insurance company, and our business partners and firm managers. Through the consortium of counsel, we gained collective wisdom that enabled us to avoid a lawsuit by settling prior to going to court. **We kept the peace** with all parties, avoiding what could have been an extensive, time-consuming, and painful situation.

Since then, we have referred to that incident as "a business development blessing in disguise." We have profited from a continuing strong relationship with our wonderful client. I stand amazed at the unmerited blessings we have received by living according to the business principles of Proverbs—even before we recognized them as such.

Clearly, God has chosen to bless our business. My stewardship journey has shown me that what looks simple on the surface is more complex in practice. I've had to go through the process of becoming a servant of the Lord, giving up the rights to my assets. This meant tearing my heart away from my money. Once I realized I was simply a manager of what had been entrusted to me, I saw the importance of transferring ownership of my stuff to its rightful owner.

I am convinced that God blesses companies, not because we deserve it or for our consumption, but for the purpose of stewardship. Because he has entrusted some of his resources to me as a business owner, I will one day stand before him to give an accounting of how I have managed the assets entrusted to my care.

I have learned to fear the Lord with a healthy fear of accountability. I desire to love and please him, and I dare not disappoint him by being an unfaithful steward. I do not have the "right" to do whatever I want with my money or assets. A faithful steward or manager gives up those rights. The final exhortation in the book of Proverbs is for wealth and influence to be used for the benefit of the poor and others on God's heart (31:8-9). The greater my generosity, the greater my opportunity to serve others. Any philanthropist can easily give money. Effective stewarding entails entrusting God's assets to other faithful stewards for multiplication. Obedience to the promptings of the Holy Spirit and God's written Word is more important than the amount given.

I've also realized I must give over my time, my talents, and my "essence," because without these, simple gifts of money are often not effective. By combining my talents, time, and money, I become available to be used by God as an effective, faithful steward. The key is obedience.

I consider the wisdom and prudence offered in the book of Proverbs to be a concentrated guidebook for young business-men and women. I am convinced we should avoid the things God warns us about and do the things God loves. Our "doing" should include seeking his treasures, being disciplined to obey his commands, and developing habits that will help us become men and women of righteous character. This righteous charac-ter will be transported into eternity though our transformed hearts.

In the future, we may have the privilege of standing up publicly for our faith in a way that risks our earthly life. Religious freedoms in the world will erode, and being a faithful follower of Jesus Christ may have a cost beyond anything we've ever experienced. If your heart were on trial for operating a business in God's economy, would there be enough evidence to convict you of being wise, humble, honest, prudent, and diligent? May it be so.

ABOUT THE AUTHOR

For over thirty-five years Raymond H. Harris, AIA, has practiced architecture. Established in 1983, his firm specializes in corporate architecture and is ranked as one of the largest firms in the United States.

Raymond graduated first in his class from the University of Oklahoma with a bachelor of science with distinction, bachelor of architecture with distinction, and master of architecture. He was selected as the outstanding senior in the College of Architecture.

He has served on numerous boards, including Crown Financial Ministries, University of Oklahoma College of Architecture, OMF International (formerly China Inland Mission), and Student Mobilization Ministries. Raymond has traveled extensively around the world and been involved with community development and transformation efforts among the poor.

Raymond has hiked all of the continental U.S. national parks and served as a Boy Scout scoutmaster for thirteen years. He received the Boy Scouts of America Silver Beaver Award for his efforts in establishing a troop at Buckner Children's Home in Dallas, Texas.

Raymond and his wife, Marydel, are blessed by their four adult children and two grandchildren.